W9-AJU-044

THE FOLGER LIBRARY SHAKESPEARE

Designed to make Shakespeare's classic plays available to the general reader, each edition contains a reliable text with modernized spelling and punctuation, scene-by-scene plot summaries, and explanatory notes clarifying obscure and obsolete expressions. An interpretive essay and accounts of Shakespeare's life and theater form an instructive preface to each play.

Louis B. Wright, General Editor, was the Director of the Folger Shakespeare Library from 1948 until his retirement in 1968. He is the author of *Middle-Class Culture in Elizabethan England, Religion and Empire, Shakespeare for Everyman,* and many other books and essays on the history and literature of the Tudor and Stuart periods.

Virginia Lamar, Assistant Editor, served as research assistant to the Director and Executive Secretary of the Folger Shakespeare Library from 1946 until her death in 1968. She is the author of *English Dress in the Age of Shakespeare* and *Travel and Roads in England,* and coeditor of William Strachey's *Historie of Travell into Virginia Britania.*

The Folger Shakespeare Library

The Folger Shakespeare Library in Washington, D.C., a research institute founded and endowed by Henry Clay Folger and administered by the Trustees of Amherst College, contains the world's largest collection of Shakespeareana. Although the Folger Library's primary purpose is to encourage advanced research in history and literature, it has continually exhibited a profound concern in stimulating a popular interest in the Elizabethan period.

GENERAL EDITOR

LOUIS B. WRIGHT

Director, Folger Shakespeare Library, 1948–1968

ASSISTANT EDITOR

VIRGINIA A. LaMAR

Executive Secretary, Folger Shakespeare Library, 1946–1968

All's Well That Ends Well

by

William Shakespeare

WASHINGTON SQUARE PRESS
PUBLISHED BY POCKET BOOKS

New York   London   Toronto   Sydney   Tokyo   Singapore

A Washington Square Press Publication of
POCKET BOOKS, a division of Simon & Schuster Inc.
1230 Avenue of the Americas, New York, NY 10020

ISBN: 0-671-66923-0

First Pocket Books printing September 1965

15 14 13 12 11 10 9 8 7 6

Preface

This edition of *All's Well That Ends Well* is designed to make available a readable text of one of Shakespeare's so-called "problem" comedies. In the centuries since Shakespeare, many changes have occurred in the meanings of words, and some clarification of Shakespeare's vocabulary may be helpful. To provide the reader with necessary notes in the most accessible format, we have placed them on the pages facing the text that they explain. We have tried to make these notes as brief and simple as possible. Preliminary to the text we have also included a brief statement of essential information about Shakespeare and his stage. Readers desiring more detailed information should refer to the books suggested in the references, and if still further information is needed, the bibliographies in those books will provide the necessary clues to the literature of the subject.

The early texts of Shakespeare's plays provide only scattered stage directions and no indications of setting, and it is conventional for modern editors to add these to clarify the action. Such additions, and additions to entrances and exits, as well as many indications of act and scene division, are placed in square brackets.

All illustrations are from material in the Folger Library collections.

L. B. W.
V. A. L.

November 16, 1964

ALL'S WELL THAT ENDS WELL

this and therefore does not conform with our expectations. We are disappointed to realize that Shakes-

Old Elements in a New Comedy

When Shakespeare put together *All's Well That Ends Well,* he utilized motifs and themes that already had an ancient tradition in folk tales and popular drama. Elements that a modern audience finds too implausible for acceptance did not bother the Elizabethan spectators at the performance of Shakespeare's play. They were familiar with folk stories and popular romances that dealt with impossible situations such as miraculous and instant cures, sudden conversions from hatred to love, tricks like the substitution of Helena for Diana in Bertram's bed, episodes involving the lack of recognition of a wife by a husband or vice versa, and a score of other unrealistic incidents, commonplaces of folk romance that Elizabethans and their predecessors had long accepted and that dramatists frequently worked into their stage plays. Accustomed as they were to conventional absurdities, it would not occur to most Elizabethan readers or spectators of a play to question the implausibilities in the plot of *All's Well That Ends Well,* which Shakespeare took from a popular tale in Boccaccio's *Decameron.*

We find this play puzzling and unsatisfactory because it is unlike other Shakespearean plays that deal more realistically with themes and situations that are universal and timeless; we are perplexed and unhappy when we find one that does not do this and therefore does not comport with our sentiments. We are disappointed to realize that Shakespeare was writing for an Elizabethan audience, not for us, an Elizabethan audience conditioned to a different set of literary and theatrical conventions.

Much of our bewilderment over the characterization and the situations in *All's Well That Ends Well* might be overcome if we would interpret the play as the Elizabethans saw it instead of trying to see it through the eyes of Coleridge or of later Victorian critics. Bertram, for example, was not a young man who would please Matthew Arnold, but he was a familiar type in the folk romances that Elizabethan apprentices devoured.

The traditions of the old morality play were still strong in the Elizabethan theatre when Shakespeare was writing. Marlowe had used the theme of the struggle of the good and evil angels for the soul of Faustus in his play, and this struggle was a commonplace in Elizabethan drama. From the time of the performance of *Everyman*, and before, audiences had learned to expect in many a drama a long-drawn-out and sometimes picturesque struggle between Good and Evil for the protagonist. Shakespeare was familiar with this well-worn tradition, which he found convenient to use once more in *All's Well*.

Bertram, whom the Victorian critics roundly damned, is the protagonist, if not exactly a hero in the modern sense. His evil genius is Parolles, the traditional braggart soldier as old as Roman comedy, who also has the qualities of the parasite and wicked counselor. Helena represents the good angel of the morality plays, who struggles for the soul of Bertram and at last wins. When the play ends, the Elizabethan audience is assured that Bertram will henceforth be a new man, a happy husband, and a worthy father. More than one hero of romance had undergone such a sudden transformation without seeming incredible. Characters in romance, and in the drama derived from similar sources, moved in a never-never land where the realities of the everyday world were not required or necessarily expected.

All's Well That Ends Well is generally classified as one of Shakespeare's "problem comedies," or sometimes as one of the "dark comedies," because it deals with a theme distasteful to modern readers and lacks the verve and sparkle of festive comedies like *As You Like It* and *A Midsummer Night's Dream.* Chronologically it falls probably between *Troilus and Cressida,* another puzzling play, and *Measure for Measure.* The best evidence gives a date of 1602–03 as the most probable time of first performance. This would place it only about two years after the first performance of *Hamlet* and two to four years before such great tragedies as *Othello, King Lear,* and *Macbeth.*

This period in Shakespeare's life was not a time that demonstrated in his work a vein of overflowing merriment, but it is not necessary to predicate some tragic obsession from personal experience that caused him to write as he did. Nevertheless, the somber tones of *All's Well That Ends Well* and *Measure for Measure* have suggested to even so judicious a scholar as Sir Edmund Chambers that the explanation must lie in some fact in Shake-

speare's life that caused him at this time to be
"working in an abnormal mood."

The tone of the play is clearly not one of gaiety
or of ebullience, but we must remember that this
was a time when tragedies were having a run of
popularity upon the Elizabethan stage, and Shakespeare was one of the principal authors of tragedies. He was writing in a "tragic vein," perhaps not
because of any deep emotional turmoil within himself, but because that was the mood of the moment
among playwrights. If we recall runs of plays in the
theatres of our own time, we can discern trends
that reflect current popularity rather than emotional stresses in the playwrights' souls. During a
period when tragedies occupied most of Shakespeare's thought, it would be natural for non-tragic
plays written at the time to reflect some of the author's thinking about the more serious and the sad-
der relationships between men and women. If the
managers of the Globe demanded a comedy at this
time, Shakespeare could hardly turn off as one turns
a spigot his reflections on tragic aspects of life and
turn on a fount of merriment. The managers would
have to be content with *All's Well That Ends Well*
and *Measure for Measure*, for that is what they got.

Literary critics, particularly critics of Shakespeare, too often forget the exigencies of the playhouse when discussing the qualities of drama. This
is especially true of Shakespeare's problem comedies. If we had a more detailed knowledge of the
personnel of the company at the Globe in 1602–03,
we might understand better the lines written for
Lavatch, the clown; Lafew, the old lord; and Parolles, the braggart soldier. These are all sure-

fire parts in the hands of competent character actors, and it is obvious that Shakespeare, himself one of the acting company, was creating these parts to capitalize upon the skills of particular individuals well known to him. Lavatch's lines are often less than funny to a modern reader, for much humor and clownery, like wine, spoils with time, but the particular clown for whom Shakespeare created the part undoubtedly got more out of the lines than we can see in them today. Similarly, Lafew's part was a favorite with Shakespeare, who created many garrulous old men, Polonius being only the best known of these comic roles. The braggart Parolles, parading in his finery and swathed in fancy scarves, was perhaps played by the same actor who two or three years before had made a success out of the part of Malvolio in *Twelfth Night*. Shakespeare, as a practical man of the theatre, was thinking more about the success of his play as interpreted by the personnel then available than he was about what critics in the age of Coleridge, or of our own time, would think of the lines that he put into his characters' mouths.

The interpretations of Helena and Bertram, heroine and "hero" of *All's Well That Ends Well*, have troubled those literary critics who insist upon thinking of the play as a representation of life rather than as a collection of motifs from traditional prose romances. In general, the critics, beginning with Coleridge, have seen in Helena a noble woman, swept away by love of an unworthy man, a situation not unknown in real life. Coleridge even went so far as to assert that Helena is Shakespeare's "loveliest character." Others were concerned at her apparent forwardness in pursuing Bertram when it was obvious that he did not want her. At last John Masefield, reacting completely against her, declared that Helena, womanlike, for her own selfish ends, put Bertram in a "position of ignominy quite unbearable." But Masefield, in a cynical mood himself, declared that she would be for all time "beloved . . . by the conventionally minded of both sexes." Despite Masefield, George Bernard Shaw, whom few would describe as "conventionally minded," admired Helena, and Shakespeare's heroine may have supplied some inspiration for Shaw's Ann Whitefield, who successfully pursues her man in *Man and Superman.*

Although Masefield believed that Shakespeare in a moment of misogyny had created Helena to portray a woman artfully contriving to capture her man, few have had a good word to say for the object of Helena's pursuit, Bertram, the elusive husband. Dr. Samuel Johnson described him as a "man noble without generosity and young without truth; who marries Helena as a coward and leaves her as a profligate; when she is dead by his unkindness, sneaks home to a second marriage, is accused by a woman whom he has wronged, defends himself by falsehood, and is dismissed to happiness." Thus does Dr. Johnson dispose of Bertram.

The interpretation of the difficult relationship between the two main characters has led to a hopeless confusion among critics as to the meaning of the play. Explanations almost as numerous as the critics themselves have been proposed, from involved allegories of the life of man, to the psychological diagnosis of the author at the time of composition. Some critics have simply thrown up their hands in despair and called the play a "fanciful imbroglio" without reality, whose characters need not be taken seriously as reflections of anything in life.

The best explanation of the play seems to be that Shakespeare, writing on demand, turned to a ready plot source and transformed a folk tale into a play suitable for the actors then popular at the Globe. It is doubtful whether he intended to lard the play with profound and esoteric meaning. It is obviously a mosaic of old themes, popular since the days of the morality play, and it undoubtedly gave pleasure to spectators, who did not come to the Globe to be instructed in morality or philosophy.

In *All's Well That Ends Well* there are evidences of haste and superficiality not often found in Shakespeare. The verse shows carelessness and is frequently stilted and wooden, to such a degree that a few scholars have seen in the play another's handiwork.

The source is the story of "Giglietta di Nerbona," the ninth story of the third day, in Boccaccio's *Decameron*. It was translated and included by William Painter in *The Palace of Pleasure* (1566), where Shakespeare could easily have read it. Shakespeare modified the story to suit his purposes, including the blackening of Bertram's character and other changes.

The play was first printed in the First Folio of 1623, and upon that text the present edition is based. The copy for the Folio version of the play shows evidence of having been a playhouse text, probably the author's own holograph.

Little evidence remains of the stage history of

this play in the seventeenth century. If it was revived after the reopening of the theatres in 1660, all evidence of the fact has vanished. Near the middle of the eighteenth century it began to attract attention. A performance took place in London in Goodman's Fields in 1741, and the next year it had a run of ten performances at Drury Lane. Peg Woffington created some interest in the role of Helena. From this time onward, the play was frequently acted. In 1832 a musical version was performed at Covent Garden. During the nineteenth and twentieth centuries the play has appeared fairly regularly in the repertory of Shakespearean companies. Audiences have never regarded it as one of their favorite plays, but it has managed to create sufficient interest to warrant production on numerous occasions.

THE AUTHOR

As early as 1598 Shakespeare was so well known as a literary and dramatic craftsman that Francis Meres, in his *Palladis Tamia: Wits Treasury*, referred in flattering terms to him as "mellifluous and honey-tongued Shakespeare," famous for his *Venus and Adonis*, his *Lucrece*, and "his sugared sonnets," which were circulating "among his private friends." Meres observes further that "as Plautus and Seneca are accounted the best for comedy and tragedy among the Latins, so Shakespeare among the English is the most excellent in both kinds for the stage," and he mentions a dozen plays that had made a name for Shakespeare. He concludes with the remark that "the Muses would speak with

Shakespeare's fine filed phrase if they would speak English."

To those acquainted with the history of the Elizabethan and Jacobean periods, it is incredible that anyone should be so naïve or ignorant as to doubt the reality of Shakespeare as the author of the plays that bear his name. Yet so much nonsense has been written about other "candidates" for the plays that it is well to remind readers that no credible evidence that would stand up in a court of law has ever been adduced to prove either that Shakespeare did not write his plays or that anyone else wrote them. All the theories offered for the authorship of Francis Bacon, the Earl of Derby, the Earl of Oxford, the Earl of Hertford, Christopher Marlowe, and a score of other candidates are mere conjectures spun from the active imaginations of persons who confuse hypothesis and conjecture with evidence.

As Meres's statement of 1598 indicates, Shakespeare was already a popular playwright whose name carried weight at the box office. The obvious reputation of Shakespeare as early as 1598 makes the effort to prove him a myth one of the most absurd in the history of human perversity.

The anti-Shakespeareans talk darkly about a plot of vested interests to maintain the authorship of Shakespeare. Nobody has any vested interest in Shakespeare, but every scholar is interested in the truth and in the quality of evidence advanced by special pleaders who set forth hypotheses in place of facts.

The anti-Shakespeareans base their arguments upon a few simple premises, all of them false.

These false premises are that Shakespeare was an unlettered yokel without any schooling, that nothing is known about Shakespeare, and that only a noble lord or the equivalent in background could have written the plays. The facts are that more is known about Shakespeare than about most dramatists of his day, that he had a very good education, acquired in the Stratford Grammar School, that the plays show no evidence of profound book learning, and that the knowledge of kings and courts evident in the plays is no greater than any intelligent young man could have picked up at second hand. Most anti-Shakespeareans are naïve and betray an obvious snobbery. The author of their favorite plays, they imply, must have had a college diploma framed and hung on his study wall like the one in their dentist's office, and obviously so great a writer must have had a title or some equally significant evidence of exalted social background. They forget that genius has a way of cropping up in unexpected places and that none of the great creative writers of the world got his inspiration in a college or university course.

William Shakespeare was the son of John Shakespeare of Stratford-upon-Avon, a substantial citizen of that small but busy market town in the center of the rich agricultural county of Warwick. John Shakespeare kept a shop, what we would call a general store; he dealt in wool and other produce and gradually acquired property. As a youth, John Shakespeare had learned the trade of glover and leather worker. There is no contemporary evidence that the elder Shakespeare was a butcher, though the anti-Shakespeareans like to talk about the ignorant "butcher's boy of Stratford." Their only evidence is a statement by gossipy John Aubrey, more than a century after William Shakespeare's birth, that young William followed his father's trade, and when he killed a calf, "he would do it in a high style and make a speech." We would like to believe the story true, but Aubrey is not a very credible witness.

John Shakespeare probably continued to operate a farm at Snitterfield that his father had leased. He married Mary Arden, daughter of his father's landlord, a man of some property. The third of their eight children was William, baptized on April 26, 1564, and probably born three days before. At least, it is conventional to celebrate April 23 as his birthday.

The Stratford records give considerable information about John Shakespeare. We know that he held several municipal offices including those of alderman and mayor. In 1580 he was in some sort of legal difficulty and was fined for neglecting a summons of the Court of Queen's Bench requiring him to appear at Westminster and be bound over to keep the peace.

As a citizen and alderman of Stratford, John Shakespeare was entitled to send his son to the grammar school free. Though the records are lost, there can be no reason to doubt that this is where young William received his education. As any student of the period knows, the grammar schools provided the basic education in Latin learning and literature. The Elizabethan grammar school is not to be confused with modern grammar schools. Many cultivated men of the day received all their formal education in the grammar schools. At the universities in this period a student would have received little training that would have inspired him to be a creative writer. At Stratford young Shakespeare would have acquired a familiarity with Latin and some little knowledge of Greek. He would have read Latin authors and become acquainted with the plays of Plautus and Terence. Undoubtedly, in this period of his life he received that stimulation to read and explore for himself the world of ancient and modern history which he later utilized in his plays. The youngster who does not acquire this type of intellectual curiosity *before* college days rarely develops as a result of a college course the kind of mind Shakespeare demonstrated. His learning in books was anything but profound, but he clearly had the probing curiosity that sent him in search of information, and he had a keenness in the observation of nature and of humankind that finds reflection in his poetry.

There is little documentation for Shakespeare's boyhood. There is little reason why there should be. Nobody knew that he was going to be a dramatist about whom any scrap of information would be prized in the centuries to come. He was merely an active and vigorous youth of Stratford, perhaps assisting his father in his business, and no Boswell bothered to write down facts about him. The most important record that we have is a marriage license issued by the Bishop of Worcester on November 27, 1582, to permit William Shakespeare to marry Anne Hathaway, seven or eight years his senior; furthermore, the Bishop permitted the marriage after reading the banns only once instead of three times, evidence of the desire for haste. The need was explained on May 26, 1583, when the christening of Susanna, daughter of William and Anne Shakespeare, was recorded at Stratford. Two years later, on February 2, 1585, the records show the birth of twins to the Shakespeares, a boy and a girl who were christened Hamnet and Judith.

What William Shakespeare was doing in Stratford during the early years of his married life, or when he went to London, we do not know. It has been conjectured that he tried his hand at school-teaching, but that is a mere guess. There is a legend that he left Stratford to escape a charge of poaching in the park of Sir Thomas Lucy of Charlecote, but there is no proof of this. There is also a legend that when first he came to London he earned his living by holding horses outside a playhouse and presently was given employment inside, but there is nothing better than eighteenth-century hearsay for this. How Shakespeare broke into the London theatres as a dramatist and actor we do not know. But lack of information is not surprising, for Elizabethans did not write their autobiographies, and we know even less about the lives of many writers and some men of affairs than we know about Shakespeare. By 1592 he was so well established and popular that he incurred the envy of the dramatist and pamphleteer Robert Greene, who referred to him as an "upstart crow . . . in his own conceit the only Shake-scene in a country." From this time onward, contemporary allusions and references in legal documents enable the scholar to chart Shakespeare's career with greater accuracy than is possible with most other Elizabethan dramatists.

By 1594 Shakespeare was a member of the company of actors known as the Lord Chamberlain's Men. After the accession of James I, in 1603, the company would have the sovereign for their patron and would be known as the King's Men. During the period of its greatest prosperity, this company would have as its principal theatres the Globe and the Blackfriars. Shakespeare was both an actor and a shareholder in the company. Tradition has assigned him such acting roles as Adam in *As You Like It* and the Ghost in *Hamlet*, a modest place on the stage that suggests that he may have had other duties in the management of the company. Such conclusions, however, are based on surmise.

What we do know is that his plays were popular and that he was highly successful in his vocation. His first play may have been *The Comedy of Errors*, acted perhaps in 1591. Certainly this was one of his earliest plays. The three parts of *Henry VI* were acted sometime between 1590 and 1592. Critics are not in agreement about precisely how much Shakespeare wrote of these three plays. *Richard III* probably dates from 1593. With this play Shakespeare captured the imagination of Elizabethan audiences, then enormously interested in historical plays. With *Richard III* Shakespeare also gave an interpretation pleasing to the Tudors of the rise to power of the grandfather of Queen Elizabeth. From this time onward, Shakespeare's plays followed on the stage in rapid succession: *Titus Andronicus, The Taming of the Shrew, The Two Gentlemen of Verona, Love's Labor's Lost, Romeo and Juliet, Richard II, A Midsummer Night's Dream, King John, The Merchant of Venice, Henry IV (Parts 1 and 2), Much Ado about Nothing, Henry V, Julius Cæsar, As You Like It, Twelfth Night, Hamlet, The Merry Wives of Windsor, All's Well That Ends Well, Measure for Measure, Othello, King Lear,* and nine others that followed before Shakespeare retired completely, about 1613.

In the course of his career in London, he made enough money to enable him to retire to Stratford with a competence. His purchase on May 4, 1597, of New Place, then the second-largest dwelling in Stratford, a "pretty house of brick and timber," with a handsome garden, indicates his increasing prosperity. There his wife and children lived while he busied himself in the London theatres. The summer before he acquired New Place, his life was darkened by the death of his only son, Hamnet, a child of eleven. In May, 1602, Shakespeare purchased one hundred and seven acres of fertile farmland near Stratford and a few months later bought a cottage and garden across the alley from New Place. About 1611, he seems to have returned permanently to Stratford, for the next year a legal document refers to him as "William Shakespeare of Stratford-upon-Avon . . . gentleman." To achieve the desired appellation of gentleman, William Shakespeare had seen to it that the College of Heralds in 1596 granted his father a coat of arms. In one step he thus became a second-generation gentleman.

Shakespeare's daughter Susanna made a good match in 1607 with Dr. John Hall, a prominent and prosperous Stratford physician. His second daughter, Judith, did not marry until she was thirty-two years old, and then, under somewhat scandalous circumstances, she married Thomas Quiney, a Stratford vintner. On March 25, 1616, Shakespeare made his will, bequeathing his landed property to Susanna, £300 to Judith, certain sums to other relatives, and his second-best bed to his wife, Anne. Much has been made of the second-best bed, but the legacy probably indicates only that Anne liked that particular bed. Shakespeare, following the practice of the time, may have already arranged with Susanna for his wife's care. Finally, on April 23, 1616, the anniversary of his birth, William Shakespeare died, and he was buried on April 25 within the chancel of Trinity Church, as befitted an honored citizen. On August 6, 1623, a few months before the publication of the collected edition of Shakespeare's plays, Anne Shakespeare joined her husband in death.

THE PUBLICATION OF HIS PLAYS

During his lifetime Shakespeare made no effort to publish any of his plays, though eighteen appeared in print in single-play editions known as quartos. Some of these are corrupt versions known as "bad quartos." No quarto, so far as is known, had the author's approval. Plays were not considered "literature" any more than most radio and television scripts today are considered literature. Dramatists sold their plays outright to the theatrical companies and it was usually considered in the company's interest to keep plays from getting into print. To achieve a reputation as a man of letters, Shakespeare wrote his *Sonnets* and his narrative poems,

Venus and Adonis and *The Rape of Lucrece*, but he probably never dreamed that his plays would establish his reputation as a literary genius. Only Ben Jonson, a man known for his colossal conceit, had the crust to call his plays *Works*, as he did when he published an edition in 1616. But men laughed at Ben Jonson.

After Shakespeare's death, two of his old colleagues in the King's Men, John Heminges and Henry Condell, decided that it would be a good thing to print, in more accurate versions than were then available, the plays already published and eighteen additional plays not previously published in quarto. In 1623 appeared *Mr. William Shakespeares Comedies, Histories, & Tragedies. Published according to the True Original Copies. London. Printed by Isaac Iaggard and Ed. Blount.* This was the famous First Folio, a work that had the authority of Shakespeare's associates. The only play commonly attributed to Shakespeare that was omitted in the First Folio was *Pericles*. In their preface, "To the great Variety of Readers," Heminges and Condell state that whereas "you were abused with diverse stolen and surreptitious copies, maimed and deformed by the frauds and stealths of injurious impostors that exposed them, even those are now offered to your view cured and perfect of their limbs; and all the rest, absolute in their numbers, as he conceived them." What they used for printer's copy is one of the vexed problems of scholarship, and skilled bibliographers have devoted years of study to the question of the relation of the "copy" for the First Folio to Shakespeare's manuscripts. In some cases it is clear that the editors corrected printed quarto versions of the plays, probably by comparison with playhouse scripts. Whether these scripts were in Shakespeare's autograph is anybody's guess. No manuscript of any play in Shakespeare's handwriting has survived. Indeed, very few play manuscripts from this period by any author are extant. The Tudor and Stuart periods had not yet learned to prize autographs and author's original manuscripts.

Since the First Folio contains eighteen plays not previously printed, it is the only source for these. For the other eighteen, which had appeared in quarto versions, the First Folio also has the authority of an edition prepared and overseen by Shakespeare's colleagues and professional associates. But since editorial standards in 1623 were far from strict, and Heminges and Condell were actors rather than editors by profession, the texts are sometimes careless. The printing and proofreading of the First Folio also left much to be desired, and some garbled passages have had to be corrected and emended. The "good quarto" texts have to be taken into account in preparing a modern edition.

Because of the great popularity of Shakespeare through the centuries, the First Folio has become a prized book, but it is not a very rare one, for it is estimated that 238 copies are extant. The Folger Shakespeare Library in Washington, D.C., has seventy-nine copies of the First Folio, collected by the founder, Henry Clay Folger, who believed that a collation of as many texts as possible would reveal significant facts about the text of Shakespeare's plays. Dr. Charlton Hinman, using an ingenious machine of his own invention for mechanical collating, has made many discoveries that throw light on Shakespeare's text and on printing practices of the day.

The probability is that the First Folio of 1623 had an edition of between 1,000 and 1,250 copies. It is believed that it sold for £1, which made it an expensive book, for £1 in 1623 was equivalent to something between $40 and $50 in modern purchasing power.

During the seventeenth century, Shakespeare was sufficiently popular to warrant three later editions in folio size, the Second Folio of 1632, the Third Folio of 1663-1664, and the Fourth Folio of 1685. The Third Folio added six other plays ascribed to Shakespeare, but these are apocryphal.

THE SHAKESPEAREAN THEATRE

The theatres in which Shakespeare's plays were performed were vastly different from those we know today. The stage was a platform that jutted out into the area now occupied by the first rows of seats on the main floor, what is called the "orchestra" in America and the "pit" in England. This platform had no curtain to come down at the ends of acts and scenes. And although simple stage properties were available, the Elizabethan theatre lacked both the machinery and the elaborate movable scenery of the modern theatre. In the rear of the platform stage was a curtained area that could be used as an inner room, a tomb, or any such scene that might be required. A balcony above this inner room, and perhaps balconies on the sides of the stage, could represent the upper deck of a ship, the entry to

Juliet's room, or a prison window. A trap door in the stage provided an entrance for ghosts and devils from the nether regions, and a similar trap in the canopied structure over the stage, known as the "heavens," made it possible to let down angels on a rope. These primitive stage arrangements help to account for many elements in Elizabethan plays. For example, since there was no curtain, the dramatist frequently felt the necessity of writing into his play action to clear the stage at the ends of acts and scenes. The funeral march at the end of *Hamlet* is not there merely for atmosphere; Shakespeare had to get the corpses off the stage. The lack of scenery also freed the dramatist from undue concern about the exact location of his sets, and the physical relation of his various settings to each other did not have to be worked out with the same precision as in the modern theatre.

Before London had buildings designed exclusively for theatrical entertainment, plays were given in inns and taverns. The characteristic inn of the period had an inner courtyard with rooms opening onto balconies overlooking the yard. Players could set up their temporary stages at one end of the yard and audiences could find seats on the balconies out of the weather. The poorer sort could stand or sit on the cobblestones in the yard, which was open to the sky. The first theatres followed this construction, and throughout the Elizabethan period the large public theatres had a yard in front of the stage open to the weather, with two or three tiers of covered balconies extending around the theatre. This physical structure again influenced the writing of plays. Because a dramatist wanted the actors to be

heard, he frequently wrote into his play orations
that could be delivered with declamatory effect. He
also provided spectacle, buffoonery, and broad jests
to keep the riotous groundlings in the yard entertained and quiet.

In another respect the Elizabethan theatre differed greatly from ours. It had no actresses. All
women's roles were taken by boys, sometimes re-
cruited from the boys' choirs of the London
churches. Some of these youths acted their roles
with great skill and the Elizabethans did not seem
to be aware of any incongruity. The first actresses
on the professional English stage appeared after
the Restoration of Charles II, in 1660, when exiled
Englishmen brought back from France practices of
the French stage.

London in the Elizabethan period, as now, was
the center of theatrical interest, though wandering
actors from time to time traveled through the country performing in inns, halls, and the houses of the
nobility. The first professional playhouse, called
simply The Theatre, was erected by James Burbage, father of Shakespeare's colleague Richard
Burbage, in 1576 on lands of the old Holywell
Priory adjacent to Finsbury Fields, a playground
and park area just north of the city walls. It had the
advantage of being outside the city's jurisdiction
and yet was near enough to be easily accessible.
Soon after The Theatre was opened, another playhouse called The Curtain was erected in the same
neighborhood. Both of these playhouses had open
courtyards and were probably polygonal in shape.

About the time The Curtain opened, Richard
Farrant, Master of the Children of the Chapel

Royal at Windsor and of St. Paul's, conceived the idea of opening a "private" theatre in the old monastery buildings of the Blackfriars, not far from St. Paul's Cathedral in the heart of the city. This theatre was ostensibly to train the choirboys in plays for presentation at Court, but Farrant managed to present plays to paying audiences and achieved considerable success until aristocratic neighbors complained and had the theatre closed. This first Blackfriars Theatre was significant, however, because it popularized the boy actors in a professional way and it paved the way for a second theatre in the Blackfriars, which Shakespeare's company took over more than thirty years later. By the last years of the sixteenth century, London had at least six professional theatres and still others were erected during the reign of James I.

The Globe Theatre, the playhouse that most people connect with Shakespeare, was erected early in 1599 on the Bankside, the area across the Thames from the city. Its construction had a dramatic beginning, for on the night of December 28, 1598, James Burbage's sons, Cuthbert and Richard, gathered together a crew who tore down the old theatre in Holywell and carted the timbers across the river to a site that they had chosen for a new playhouse. The reason for this clandestine operation was a row with the landowner over the lease to the Holywell property. The site chosen for the Globe was another playground outside of the city's jurisdiction, a region of somewhat unsavory character. Not far away was the Bear Garden, an amphitheatre devoted to the baiting of bears and bulls. This was also the region occupied by many houses of ill fame licensed by the Bishop of Winchester and the source of substantial revenue to him. But it was easily accessible either from London Bridge or by means of the cheap boats operated by the London watermen, and it had the great advantage of being beyond the authority of the Puritanical aldermen of London, who frowned on plays because they lured apprentices from work, filled their heads with improper ideas, and generally exerted a bad influence. The aldermen also complained that the crowds drawn together in the theatre helped to spread the plague.

The Globe was the handsomest theatre up to its time. It was a large building, apparently octagonal in shape, and open like its predecessors to the sky in the center, but capable of seating a large audience in its covered balconies. To erect and operate the Globe, the Burbages organized a syndicate composed of the leading members of the dramatic company, of which Shakespeare was a member. Since it was open to the weather and depended on natural light, plays had to be given in the afternoon. This caused no hardship in the long afternoons of an English summer, but in the winter the weather was a great handicap and discouraged all except the hardiest. For that reason, in 1608 Shakespeare's company was glad to take over the lease of the second Blackfriars Theatre, a substantial, roomy hall reconstructed within the framework of the old monastery building. This theatre was protected from the weather and its stage was artificially lighted by chandeliers of candles. This became the winter playhouse for Shakespeare's company and at once proved so popular that the congestion of traffic created an embarrassing problem. Stringent regulations had to be made for the movement of coaches in the vicinity. Shakespeare's company continued to use the Globe during the summer months. In 1613 a squib fired from a cannon during a performance of *Henry VIII* fell on the thatched roof and the Globe burned to the ground. The next year it was rebuilt.

London had other famous theatres. The Rose, just west of the Globe, was built by Philip Henslowe, a semiliterate denizen of the Bankside, who became one of the most important theatrical owners and producers of the Tudor and Stuart periods. What is more important for historians, he kept a detailed account book, which provides much of our information about theatrical history in his time. Another famous theatre on the Bankside was the Swan, which a Dutch priest, Johannes de Witt, visited in 1596. The crude drawing of the stage which he made was copied by his friend Arend van Buchell; it is one of the important pieces of contemporary evidence for theatrical construction. Among the other theatres, the Fortune, north of the city, on Golding Lane, and the Red Bull, even farther away from the city, off St. John's Street, were the most popular. The Red Bull, much frequented by apprentices, favored sensational and sometimes rowdy plays.

The actors who kept all of these theatres going were organized into companies under the protection of some noble patron. Traditionally actors had enjoyed a low reputation. In some of the ordinances they were classed as vagrants; in the phraseology of the time, "rogues, vagabonds, sturdy beggars, and common players" were all listed together as undesirables. To escape penalties often meted out to these characters, organized groups of actors managed to gain the protection of various personages of high degree. In the later years of Elizabeth's reign, a group flourished under the name of the Queen's Men; another group had the protection of the Lord Admiral and were known as the Lord Admiral's Men. Edward Alleyn, son-in-law of Philip Henslowe, was the leading spirit in the Lord Admiral's Men. Besides the adult companies, troupes of boy actors from time to time also enjoyed considerable popularity. Among these were the Children of Paul's and the Children of the Chapel Royal.

The company with which Shakespeare had a long association had for its first patron Henry Carey, Lord Hunsdon, the Lord Chamberlain, and hence they were known as the Lord Chamberlain's Men. After the accession of James I, they became the King's Men. This company was the great rival of the Lord Admiral's Men, managed by Henslowe and Alleyn.

All was not easy for the players in Shakespeare's time, for the aldermen of London were always eager for an excuse to close up the Blackfriars and any other theatres in their jurisdiction. The theatres outside the jurisdiction of London were not immune from interference, for they might be shut up by order of the Privy Council for meddling in politics or for various other offenses, or they might be closed in time of plague lest they spread infection. During plague times, the actors usually went on tour and played the provinces wherever they could find an audience. Particularly frightening were the plagues of 1592-1594 and 1613 when the theatres closed and the players, like many other Londoners, had to take to the country.

Though players had a low social status, they enjoyed great popularity, and one of the favorite forms of entertainment at Court was the performance of plays. To be commanded to perform at Court conferred great prestige upon a company of players, and printers frequently noted that fact when they published plays. Several of Shakespeare's plays were performed before the sovereign, and Shakespeare himself undoubtedly acted in some of these plays.

REFERENCES FOR FURTHER READING

Many readers will want suggestions for further reading about Shakespeare and his times. A few references will serve as guides to further study in the enormous literature on the subject. A simple and useful little book is Gerald Sanders, *A Shakespeare Primer* (New York, 1950). *A Companion to Shakespeare Studies,* edited by Harley Granville-Barker and G. B. Harrison (Cambridge, 1934), is a valuable guide. The most recent concise handbook of facts about Shakespeare is Gerald E. Bentley, *Shakespeare: A Biographical Handbook* (New Haven, 1961). More detailed but not so voluminous as to be confusing is Hazelton Spencer, *The Art and Life of William Shakespeare* (New York, 1940), which, like Sanders' and Bentley's handbooks, contain a brief annotated list of useful books on various aspects of the subject. The most detailed and scholarly work providing complete factual information about Shakespeare is Sir Edmund Chambers, *William Shakespeare: A Study of Facts and Problems* (2 vols., Oxford, 1930).

Among other biographies of Shakespeare, Joseph Quincy Adams, *A Life of William Shakespeare* (Boston, 1923) is still an excellent assessment of the essential facts and the traditional information, and Marchette Chute, *Shakespeare of London* (New York, 1949; paperback, 1957) stresses Shakespeare's life in the theatre. Two new biographies of Shakespeare have recently appeared. A. L. Rowse, *William Shakespeare: A Biography* (London, 1963; New York, 1964) provides an appraisal by a distinguished English historian, who dismisses the notion that somebody else wrote Shakespeare's plays as arrant nonsense that runs counter to known historical fact. Peter Quennell, *Shakespeare: A Biography* (Cleveland and New York, 1963) is a sensitive and intelligent survey of what is known and surmised of Shakespeare's life. Louis B. Wright, *Shakespeare for Everyman* (paperback; New York, 1964) discusses the basis of Shakespeare's enduring popularity.

The Shakespeare Quarterly, published by the Shakespeare Association of America under the editorship of James G. McManaway, is recommended for those who wish to keep up with current Shakespearean scholarship and stage productions. The *Quarterly* includes an annual bibliography of Shakespeare editions and works on Shakespeare published during the previous year.

The question of the authenticity of Shakespeare's plays arouses perennial attention. The theory of hidden cryptograms in the plays is demolished by William F. and Elizebeth S. Friedman, *The Shakespearean Ciphers Examined* (New York, 1957). A succinct account of the various absurdities advanced to suggest the authorship of a multitude of candidates other than Shakespeare will be found in R. C. Churchill, *Shakespeare and His Betters* (Bloomington, Ind., 1959). Another recent discussion of the subject, *The Authorship of Shakespeare*, by James G. McManaway (Washington, D.C., 1962), presents the evidence from contemporary records to prove the identity of Shakespeare the actor-playwright with Shakespeare of Stratford.

Scholars are not in agreement about the details of playhouse construction in the Elizabethan period. John C. Adams presents a plausible reconstruction of the Globe in *The Globe Playhouse: Its Design and Equipment* (Cambridge, Mass., 1942; 2nd rev. ed., 1961). A description with excellent drawings based on Dr. Adams' model is Irwin Smith, *Shakespeare's Globe Playhouse: A Modern Reconstruction in Text and Scale Drawings* (New York, 1956). Other sensible discussions are C. Walter Hodges, *The Globe Restored* (London, 1953) and A. M. Nagler, *Shakespeare's Stage* (New Haven, 1958). Bernard Beckerman, *Shakespeare at the Globe, 1599–1609* (New Haven, 1962; paperback, 1962) discusses Elizabethan staging and acting techniques.

A sound and readable history of the early theatres is Joseph Quincy Adams, *Shakespearean Playhouses: A History of English Theatres from the Beginnings to the Restoration* (Boston, 1917). For detailed, factual information about the Elizabethan and seventeenth-century stages, the definitive reference works are Sir Edmund Chambers, *The Elizabethan Stage* (4 vols., Oxford, 1923) and Gerald E. Bentley, *The Jacobean and Caroline Stages* (5 vols., Oxford, 1941–1956).

Further information on the history of the theatre and related topics will be found in the following titles: T. W. Baldwin, *The Organization and Personnel of the Shakespearean Company* (Princeton, 1927); Lily Bess Campbell, *Scenes and Machines on the English Stage during the Renaissance* (Cambridge, 1923); Esther Cloudman Dunn, *Shakespeare in America* (New York, 1939); George C. D. Odell, *Shakespeare from Betterton to Irving* (2 vols., London, 1931); Arthur Colby Sprague, *Shakespeare and the Actors: The Stage Business in His Plays (1660–1905)* (Cambridge, Mass., 1944) and *Shakespearian Players and Performances* (Cambridge, Mass., 1953); Leslie Hotson, *The Commonwealth and Restoration Stage* (Cambridge, Mass., 1928); Alwin Thaler, *Shakspere to Sheridan: A Book about the Theatre of Yesterday and To-day* (Cambridge, Mass., 1922); George C. Branam, *Eighteenth-Century Adaptations of Shakespeare's Tragedies* (Berkeley, 1956); C. Beecher Hogan, *Shakespeare in the Theatre, 1701–1800* (Oxford, 1957); Ernest Bradlee Watson, *Sheridan to Robertson: A Study of the 19th-Century London Stage* (Cambridge, Mass., 1926); and Enid Welsford, *The Court Masque* (Cambridge, Mass., 1927).

A brief account of the growth of Shakespeare's reputation is F. E. Halliday, *The Cult of Shakespeare* (London, 1947). A more detailed discussion is given in Augustus Ralli, *A History of Shakespearian Criticism* (2 vols., Oxford, 1932; New York,

1958). Harley Granville-Barker, *Prefaces to Shakespeare* (5 vols., London, 1927–1948; 2 vols., London, 1958) provides stimulating critical discussion of the plays. An older classic of criticism is Andrew C. Bradley, *Shakespearean Tragedy: Lectures on Hamlet, Othello, King Lear, Macbeth* (London, 1904; paperback, 1955). Sir Edmund Chambers, *Shakespeare: A Survey* (London, 1935; paperback, 1958) contains short, sensible essays on thirty-four of the plays, originally written as introductions to single-play editions.

For the history plays see Lily Bess Campbell, *Shakespeare's "Histories": Mirrors of Elizabethan Policy* (Cambridge, 1947); John Palmer, *Political Characters of Shakespeare* (London, 1945; 1961); E. M. W. Tillyard, *Shakespeare's History Plays* (London, 1948); Irving Ribner, *The English History Play in the Age of Shakespeare* (Princeton, 1947); and Max M. Reese, *The Cease of Majesty* (London, 1961).

The comedies are illuminated by the following studies: C. L. Barber, *Shakespeare's Festive Comedy* (Princeton, 1959); John Russell Brown, *Shakespeare and His Comedies* (London, 1957); H. B. Charlton, *Shakespearian Comedy* (London, 1938; 4th ed., 1949); W. W. Lawrence, *Shakespeare's Problem Comedies* (New York, 1931); and Thomas M. Parrott, *Shakespearean Comedy* (New York, 1949).

In addition to the general works on Shakespeare's comedies cited above, *All's Well That Ends Well* is discussed in E. M. W. Tillyard, *Shakespeare's Problem Plays* (London, 1950). The edition of the play by G. K. Hunter in the new Arden series (London,

1959) has a comprehensive introduction and re-prints William Painter's version of the source tale from Boccaccio.

Further discussions of Shakespeare's tragedies, in addition to Bradley, already cited, are contained in H. B. Charlton, *Shakespearian Tragedy* (Cambridge, 1948); Willard Farnham, *The Medieval Heritage of Elizabethan Tragedy* (Berkeley, 1936) and *Shakespeare's Tragic Frontier: The World of His Final Tragedies* (Berkeley, 1950); and Harold S. Wilson, *On the Design of Shakespearian Tragedy* (Toronto, 1957).

The "Roman" plays are treated in M. M. MacCallum, *Shakespeare's Roman Plays and Their Background* (London, 1910) and J. C. Maxwell, "Shakespeare's Roman Plays, 1900–1956," *Shakespeare Survey 10* (Cambridge, 1957), 1-11.

Kenneth Muir, *Shakespeare's Sources: Comedies and Tragedies* (London, 1957) discusses Shakespeare's use of source material. The sources themselves have been reprinted several times. Among old editions are John P. Collier (ed.), *Shakespeare's Library* (2 vols., London, 1850), Israel C. Gollancz (ed.), *The Shakespeare Classics* (12 vols., London, 1907–26), and W. C. Hazlitt (ed.), *Shakespeare's Library* (6 vols., London, 1875). A modern edition is being prepared by Geoffrey Bullough with the title *Narrative and Dramatic Sources of Shakespeare* (London and New York, 1957–). Five volumes, covering the sources for the comedies, histories and Roman plays, have been published to date (1965).

In addition to the second edition of *Webster's New International Dictionary*, which contains most of the unusual words used by Shakespeare, the following reference works are helpful: Edwin A. Abbott, *A Shakespearian Grammar* (London, 1872); C. T. Onions, *A Shakespeare Glossary* (2nd rev. ed., Oxford, 1925); and Eric Partridge, *Shakespeare's Bawdy* (New York, 1948, paperback, 1960).

Some knowledge of the social background of the period in which Shakespeare lived is important for a full understanding of his work. A brief, clear, and accurate account of Tudor history is S. T. Bindoff, *The Tudors*, in the Penguin series. A readable general history is G. M. Trevelyan, *The History of England*, first published in 1926 and available in numerous editions. The same author's *English Social History*, first published in 1942 and also available in many editions, provides fascinating information about England in all periods. Sir John Neale, *Queen Elizabeth* (London, 1935; paperback, 1957) is the best study of the great Queen. Various aspects of life in the Elizabethan period are treated in Louis B. Wright, *Middle-Class Culture in Elizabethan England* (Chapel Hill, N.C., 1935; reprinted Ithaca, N.Y., 1958, 1964). *Shakespeare's England: An Account of the Life and Manners of His Age*, edited by Sidney Lee and C. T. Onions (2 vols., Oxford, 1917), provides much information on many aspects of Elizabethan life. A fascinating survey of the period will be found in Muriel St. C. Byrne, *Elizabethan Life in Town and Country* (London, 1925; rev. ed., 1954; paperback, 1961).

The Folger Library is issuing a series of illustrated booklets entitled "Folger Booklets on Tudor and Stuart Civilization," printed and distributed by Cornell University Press. Published to date are the following titles:

D. W. Davies, *Dutch Influences on English Culture, 1558-1625*

Giles E. Dawson, *The Life of William Shakespeare*

Ellen C. Eyler, *Early English Gardens and Garden Books*

John R. Hale, *The Art of War and Renaissance England*

William Haller, *Elizabeth I and the Puritans*

Virginia A. LaMar, *English Dress in the Age of Shakespeare*

——, *Travel and Roads in England*

John L. Lievsay, *The Elizabethan Image of Italy*

James G. McManaway, *The Authorship of Shakespeare*

Dorothy E. Mason, *Music in Elizabethan England*

Garrett Mattingly, *The "Invincible" Armada and Elizabethan England*

Boies Penrose, *Tudor and Early Stuart Voyaging*

Conyers Read, *The Government of England under Elizabeth*

Albert J. Schmidt, *The Yeoman in Tudor and Stuart England*

Lilly C. Stone, *English Sports and Recreations*

Craig R. Thompson, *The Bible in English, 1525-1611*

——, *The English Church in the Sixteenth Century*

——, *Schools in Tudor England*

——, *Universities in Tudor England*

Louis B. Wright, *Shakespeare's Theatre and the Dramatic Tradition*

At intervals the Folger Library plans to gather these booklets in hardbound volumes. The first is

Life and Letters in Tudor and Stuart England, First Folger Series, edited by Louis B. Wright and Virginia A. LaMar (published for the Folger Shakespeare Library by Cornell University Press, 1962). The volume contains eleven of the separate booklets.

King of France.
Duke of Florence.
Bertram, Count of Rossillion.
Lafew, an old lord.
Parolles, a follower of *Bertram.*
Rinaldo, the Steward, } servants to the *Countess of*
Lavatch, the Clown,   } *Rossillion.*
A page.
Countess of Rossillion, mother to *Bertram.*
Helena, a gentlewoman protected by the *Countess.*
An old Widow of Florence.
Diana, daughter to the *Widow.*
Mariana, neighbor and friend to the *Widow.*
Lords, Officers, Soldiers, etc., French and Florentine.

SCENE: *Rossillion; Paris; Florence; Marseilles.*]

ALL'S WELL
THAT ENDS WELL

ACT I

I. i. The Countess of Rossillion says good-by to her son, Bertram, who, since his father has died, must place himself under the guardianship of the King of France. Helena, an attendant of the Countess, has also lost her father, a famous physician, and the Countess is concerned at the severity of her grief. She does not realize that Helena's sadness is caused by her passion for Bertram and her feeling that his superior station in life makes him unobtainable. When Helena learns that the King is suffering from an ailment that his physicians have despaired of curing, she sees an opportunity to do something that may lead to the realization of her dreams.

⸻⸻⸻⸻

5. **in ward:** wealthy heirs were usually wards of the Crown until they came of age. This implies that Bertram was not yet of legal age.

7. **of:** in.

9. **hold his virtue to:** continue his goodness toward.

10. **wanted:** lacked; was lacking.

15-6, **persecuted time with hope:** i.e., made his days wearisome with treatments that offered false hopes of a cure.

ACT I

Scene I. [Rossillion. The Count's palace.]

Enter Bertram, Count of Rossillion, his mother, [the Countess], Helena, and Lord Lafew, all in black.

Coun. In delivering my son from me, I bury a second husband.

Ber. And I in going, madam, weep o'er my father's death anew; but I must attend His Majesty's command, to whom I am now in ward, evermore in 5 subjection.

Lafew. You shall find of the King a husband, madam; you, sir, a father. He that so generally is at all times good, must of necessity hold his virtue to you, whose worthiness would stir it up where it wanted, 10 rather than lack it where there is such abundance.

Coun. What hope is there of His Majesty's amendment?

Lafew. He hath abandoned his physicians, madam, under whose practices he hath persecuted time 15 with hope and finds no other advantage in the process but only the losing of hope by time.

Coun. This young gentlewoman had a father—O, that "had"! how sad a passage 'tis!—whose skill was

1

31. **still:** always.

35. **fistula:** ulcer.

43. **virtuous qualities:** accomplishments, wherein education has supplemented her natural endowments.

43-4. **commendations go with pity:** approval is accompanied by regret that it cannot be unqualified; **virtues and traitors:** that is, virtues in such circumstances are betrayals of the person's true nature.

45. **simpleness:** purity; **derives:** inherits.

46. **honesty:** honorable estate; **goodness:** preference for the good; virtuous inclination.

49. **season:** preserve.

almost as great as his honesty; had it stretched so   20
far, would have made nature immortal, and death
should have play for lack of work. Would, for the
King's sake, he were living! I think it would be the
death of the King's disease.

Lafew. How called you the man you speak of,   25
madam?

Coun. He was famous, sir, in his profession, and
it was his great right to be so: Gerard de Narbon.

Lafew. He was excellent indeed, madam. The King
very lately spoke of him admiringly and mourningly;   30
he was skillful enough to have lived still, if knowledge could be set up against mortality.

Ber. What is it, my good lord, the King languishes
of?

Lafew. A fistula, my lord.   35

Ber. I heard not of it before.

Lafew. I would it were not notorious. Was this
gentlewoman the daughter of Gerard de Narbon?

Coun. His sole child, my lord, and bequeathed to
my overlooking. I have those hopes of her good that   40
her education promises. Her dispositions she inherits,
which makes fair gifts fairer; for where an unclean
mind carries virtuous qualities, there commendations
go with pity; they are virtues and traitors too. In her
they are the better for their simpleness; she derives   45
her honesty and achieves her goodness.

Lafew. Your commendations, madam, get from her
tears.

Coun. 'Tis the best brine a maiden can season her
praise in. The remembrance of her father never ap-   50

52. **livelihood:** animation.

53. **go to:** leave off; stop.

54, 55. **affect:** (1) assume falsely; (2) incline toward, love. Helena means that her sorrow for her father's death is only a cloak to hide her real sorrow at her hopeless love for Bertram.

58-9. **If the living be enemy to the grief, the excess makes it soon mortal:** if the survivors fight against grief, grief becomes excessive and destroys itself.

64. **blood:** noble birth.

65-6. **thy goodness /Share with thy birthright:** may your own virtue equal your honorable birth.

67. **able for:** equal in competence to.

68. **keep:** guard.

69. **Under thy own life's key:** as you would your own life; **checked:** rebuked.

70. **taxed:** synonymous with **checked.**

73. **unseasoned:** inexperienced.

proaches her heart but the tyranny of her sorrows
takes all livelihood from her cheek. No more of this,
Helena, go to, no more, lest it be rather thought you
affect a sorrow than to have—

Hel. I do affect a sorrow, indeed, but I have it too.   55

Lafew. Moderate lamentation is the right of the
dead, excessive grief the enemy to the living.

Coun. If the living be enemy to the grief, the excess makes it soon mortal.

Ber. Madam, I desire your holy wishes.   60

Lafew. How understand we that?

Coun. Be thou blest, Bertram, and succeed thy
    father
In manners, as in shape! Thy blood and virtue
Contend for empire in thee, and thy goodness   65
Share with thy birthright! Love all, trust a few,
Do wrong to none: be able for thine enemy
Rather in power than use; and keep thy friend
Under thy own life's key. Be checked for silence,
But never taxed for speech. What Heaven more will,   70
That thee may furnish and my prayers pluck down,
Fall on thy head! Farewell, my lord.
'Tis an unseasoned courtier: good my lord,
Advise him.

Lafew. He cannot want the best   75
That shall attend his love.

Coun. Heaven bless him! Farewell, Bertram.

[*Exit.*]

Ber. The best wishes that can be forged in your
thoughts be servants to you! [*To Helena*] Be com-

82-3. **hold the credit:** preserve the reputation (in her own behavior).

84. **were that all:** if only that were all.

85. **grace:** honor.

88. **favor:** face; image.

90-1. **'Twere all one /That:** it's just as though.

93-4. **In his bright radiance and collateral light /Must I be comforted, not in his sphere:** continuing the astrological metaphor, Helena says that all she can hope for is the sight of his splendor, since she and Bertram move in different spheres that are **collateral** (parallel) but can never touch.

99. **hawking:** keen as a hawk's; bright.

100. **table:** notebook.

100-1. **capable /Of:** susceptible to.

101. **trick:** distinctive trait.

107. **solely:** completely.

fortable to my mother, your mistress, and make much   80
of her.

   Lafew. Farewell, pretty lady; you must hold the
credit of your father.   [*Exeunt Bertram and Lafew.*]

   Hel. O, were that all! I think not on my father;
And these great tears grace his remembrance more   85
Than those I shed for him. What was he like?
I have forgot him. My imagination
Carries no favor in't but Bertram's.
I am undone: there is no living, none,
If Bertram be away. 'Twere all one   90
That I should love a bright particular star
And think to wed it, he is so above me:
In his bright radiance and collateral light
Must I be comforted, not in his sphere.
The ambition in my love thus plagues itself: 95
The hind that would be mated by the lion
Must die for love. 'Twas pretty, though a plague,
To see him every hour; to sit and draw
His arched brows, his hawking eye, his curls,
In our heart's table—heart too capable   100
Of every line and trick of his sweet favor.
But now he's gone, and my idolatrous fancy
Must sanctify his relics. Who comes here?

             Enter Parolles.

[*Aside*] One that goes with him. I love him for his
   sake;   105
And yet I know him a notorious liar,
Think him a great way fool, solely a coward;

109-10. **they take place,** when virtue's steely bones /Looks bleak i' the cold wind: the evils (in the person of Parolles) are allowed admittance, when more virtuous persons who lack his power to please are left out in the cold.

111. **Cold:** unadorned; **superfluous:** overclothed.

112. **Save you:** God save you.

117. **Stain:** trace.

124. **setting down before:** besieging.

125. **blow you up:** get you pregnant.

133-34. **increase:** i.e., of population; **got:** begot.

135. **That:** that which.

137. **ten times found:** i.e., ten more virgins may be the result of the loss of virginity. Parolles is apparently thinking of the 10 per cent interest permitted on investments.

Yet these fixed evils sit so fit in him
That they take place, when virtue's steely bones
Looks bleak i' the cold wind. Withal, full oft we see   110
Cold wisdom waiting on superfluous folly.

Par. Save you, fair queen!

Hel. And you, monarch!

Par. No.

Hel. And no.   115

Par. Are you meditating on virginity?

Hel. Ay. You have some stain of soldier in you: let
me ask you a question. Man is enemy to virginity;
how may we barricado it against him?

Par. Keep him out.   120

Hel. But he assails; and our virginity, though valiant, in the defense yet is weak: unfold to us some
warlike resistance.

Par. There is none: man, setting down before you,
will undermine you and blow you up.   125

Hel. Bless our poor virginity from underminers and
blowers-up! Is there no military policy how virgins
might blow up men?

Par. Virginity being blown down, man will quick-
lier be blown up. Marry, in blowing him down again,   130
with the breach yourselves made, you lose your city.
It is not politic in the commonwealth of Nature to
preserve virginity. Loss of virginity is rational increase, and there was never virgin got till virginity
was first lost. That you were made of is metal to   135
make virgins. Virginity, by being once lost, may be
ten times found; by being ever kept, it is ever lost.
'Tis too cold a companion; away with't!

139. **stand for't:** defend it.

145-46. **buried in highways:** the fate of suicides.

149. **his:** its; **stomach:** pride.

151. **inhibited:** prohibited.

152. **choose but:** fail to.

158-59. **marry, ill, to like him that ne'er it likes:** verily, do evil, in loving a man who has no use for virginity and will make an end of yours.

160. **lying:** going unused.

161. **answer the time of request:** supply the demand while the demand exists.

164. **wear not:** are unfashionable; **date:** a pun on the fruit and "date of birth" (age).

Nobilis gallus ornatus

A French courtier. From Pietro Bertelli, *Diversarum nationum habitus* (1594).

Hel. I will stand for't a little, though therefor I die a virgin.   140

Par. There's little can be said in't; 'tis against the rule of nature. To speak on the part of virginity is to accuse your mothers; which is most infallible disobedience. He that hangs himself is a virgin: virginity murders itself and should be buried in high-   145
ways out of all sanctified limit, as a desperate offendress against Nature. Virginity breeds mites, much like a cheese; consumes itself to the very paring, and so dies with feeding his own stomach. Besides, virginity is peevish, proud, idle, made of self-love,   150
which is the most inhibited sin in the canon. Keep it not; you cannot choose but lose by't: out with't! Within ten year it will make itself ten, which is a goodly increase; and the principal itself not much the worse: away with't!   155

Hel. How might one do, sir, to lose it to her own liking?

Par. Let me see: marry, ill, to like him that ne'er it likes. 'Tis a commodity will lose the gloss with lying; the longer kept, the less worth. Off with't while   160
'tis vendible; answer the time of request. Virginity, like an old courtier, wears her cap out of fashion; richly suited but unsuitable, just like the brooch and the toothpick, which wear not now. Your date is better in your pie and your porridge than in your cheek: 165
and your virginity, your old virginity, is like one of our French withered pears: it looks ill, it eats drily. Marry, 'tis a withered pear; it was formerly better;

172. **There, etc.**: the abrupt transition here suggests that a line or lines may be missing.

173-79. **A mother . . . disaster**: a parody of the typical conceits of Elizabethan love poetry, in which the lover compared his mistress to the various things mentioned.

174. **phoenix**: rare bird, the only one of its kind.

180. **fond**: foolish; **adoptious christendoms**: nicknames.

181. **blinking Cupid gossips**: blind Cupid stands godfather to (sponsors).

189. **baser stars do shut us up in wishes**: inferiority limits us to wishing.

190. **with effects of them follow our friends**: serve our friends with deeds effecting the good wishes.

191. **alone must think**: can only think (but not carry out).

marry, yet 'tis a withered pear. Will you anything
with it?   170

Hel. Not my virginity yet.
There shall your master have a thousand loves,
A mother and a mistress and a friend,
A phoenix, captain, and an enemy,
A guide, a goddess, and a sovereign,   175
A counselor, a traitress, and a dear;
His humble ambition, proud humility,
His jarring concord, and his discord dulcet,
His faith, his sweet disaster; with a world
Of pretty, fond, adoptious christendoms   180
That blinking Cupid gossips. Now shall he—
I know not what he shall. God send him well!
The court's a learning place, and he is one—

Par. What one, i' faith?

Hel. That I wish well. 'Tis pity—   185

Par. What's pity?

Hel. That wishing well had not a body in't
Which might be felt; that we, the poorer born,
Whose baser stars do shut us up in wishes,
Might with effects of them follow our friends   190
And show what we alone must think, which never
Returns us thanks.

Enter Page.

Page. Monsieur Parolles, my lord calls for you.
                                                            [*Exit.*]

Par. Little Helen, farewell: if I can remember
thee, I will think of thee at court.   195

204. **retrograde:** moving backward.

209. **composition:** compound.

210. **a good wing:** swift flight.

210-11. **I like the wear well:** a satiric compliment on his dress. Flaps or rolls of fabric that covered the seams where the shoulder and sleeve joined were known as "wings." Parolles likes fantastic dress, and his "wings" were probably larger than was fashionable.

213. **acutely:** to the point; **return perfect courtier:** reply like a **perfect courtier.**

214. **naturalize thee:** make thee feel at home.

215. **capable of:** able to understand.

218. **makes thee away:** kills thee.

219-20. **when thou hast none, remember thy friends:** i.e., think of your friends only when you have no time to do anything for them.

223. **fated sky:** stars that supposedly control human fate.

The sign for the planet Mars. From *Albumasar de magnis iunctionis* (1515).

Hel. Monsieur Parolles, you were born under a charitable star.

Par. Under Mars, I.

Hel. I especially think, under Mars.

Par. Why under Mars?   200

Hel. The wars hath so kept you under that you must needs be born under Mars.

Par. When he was predominant.

Hel. When he was retrograde, I think, rather.

Par. Why think you so?   205

Hel. You go so much backward when you fight.

Par. That's for advantage.

Hel. So is running away, when fear proposes the safety: but the composition that your valor and fear makes in you is a virtue of a good wing, and I like 210 the wear well.

Par. I am so full of businesses, I cannot answer thee acutely. I will return perfect courtier; in the which my instruction shall serve to naturalize thee, so thou wilt be capable of a courtier's counsel and 215 understand what advice shall thrust upon thee; else thou diest in thine unthankfulness and thine ignorance makes thee away: farewell. When thou hast leisure, say thy prayers; when thou hast none, remember thy friends. Get thee a good husband and 220 use him as he uses thee. So, farewell.   [*Exit.*]

Hel. Our remedies oft in ourselves do lie,
Which we ascribe to Heaven: the fated sky
Gives us free scope, only doth backward pull
Our slow designs when we ourselves are dull.   225
What power is it which mounts my love so high;

227. Makes me see and cannot feed mine eye: i.e., makes me so love Bertram that the mere sight of him cannot satisfy me.

228-29. The mightiest space in fortune Nature brings /To join like likes and kiss like native things: Nature surmounts the greatest differences of fortune to join like temperament with like, as though they were of equal birth.

231. weigh their pains in sense: can imagine the difficulty of the effort.

━━━━━━━━━━━━━━━━━━━━━━━━━━━━━

I. ii. Bertram and his companion, Parolles, arrive at the French court just as the King receives news of war between the Florentines and Sienese; the King has given permission to the youthful nobility to join either side in order to gain military experience. He praises Bertram's father, whose death has been a loss to the realm. He also laments the loss of his own youth and vigor.

━━━━━━━━━━━━━━━━━━━━━━━

1. Senoys: Sienese.
3. braving: defiant.
6. our cousin Austria: the ruler of Austria.
7. move: appeal to.
12. Approved: demonstrated.

That makes me see and cannot feed mine eye?
The mightiest space in fortune Nature brings
To join like likes and kiss like native things.
Impossible be strange attempts to those   230
That weigh their pains in sense and do suppose
What hath been cannot be. Who ever strove
To show her merit that did miss her love?
The King's disease—my project may deceive me,
But my intents are fixed, and will not leave me.   235

                                        Exit.

[Scene II. Paris. The King's palace.]

*Flourish of cornets. Enter the King of France, with
      letters, and divers Attendants.*

King. The Florentines and Senoys are by the ears;
Have fought with equal fortune and continue
A braving war.
    1. Lo.   So 'tis reported, sir.
    King. Nay, 'tis most credible. We here receive it   5
A certainty, vouched from our cousin Austria,
With caution that the Florentine will move us
For speedy aid; wherein our dearest friend
Prejudicates the business and would seem
To have us make denial.   10
    1. Lo.   His love and wisdom,
Approved so to your Majesty, may plead
For amplest credence.

21. **breathing:** exercise.

26. **Frank:** generous; **curious:** meticulous.

32-3. **did look far /Into the service of the time:** had a profound understanding of contemporary military science.

34. **Discipled of:** followed by.

36. **wore us out of act:** wore out our ability to act.

40-1. **their own scorn return to them unnoted /Ere they can hide their levity in honor:** they so forget their dignity that they become objects of ridicule themselves before they realize it.

King.   He hath armed our answer,
And Florence is denied before he comes: 15
Yet, for our gentlemen that mean to see
The Tuscan service, freely have they leave
To stand on either part.

2. Lo.   It well may serve
A nursery to our gentry, who are sick   20
For breathing and exploit.

King.   What's he comes here?

Enter Bertram, Lafew, and Parolles.

1. Lo. It is the Count Rossillion, my good lord,
Young Bertram.

King.   Youth, thou bearst thy father's face;   25
Frank nature, rather curious than in haste,
Hath well composed thee. Thy father's moral parts
Mayst thou inherit too! Welcome to Paris.

Ber. My thanks and duty are your Majesty's.

King. I would I had that corporal soundness now,   30
As when thy father and myself in friendship
First tried our soldiership! He did look far
Into the service of the time and was
Discipled of the bravest. He lasted long;
But on us both did haggish age steal on   35
And wore us out of act. It much repairs me
To talk of your good father. In his youth
He had the wit which I can well observe
Today in our young lords; but they may jest
Till their own scorn return to them unnoted   40
Ere they can hide their levity in honor.

42. **contempt nor:** neither contempt nor.

45. **Clock to itself:** serving as its own watchman.

46. **Exception:** offense; objection to the conversation.

47. **His tongue obeyed his hand:** his speech was suitable to the occasion.

48. **another place:** i.e., a station above their actual place.

51. **In their poor praise he humbled:** in humbling himself to praise people of their low station.

53-4. **would demonstrate them now /But goers backward:** would show their present course to be wrong.

57-8. **So in approof lives not his epitaph /As in your royal speech:** your words more truly assert his worth than does the epitaph on his tomb.

61. **plausive:** worthy of applause; judicious.

65-6. **On the catastrophe and heel of pastime, /When it was out:** i.e., in a reflective moment after enjoying some pleasure. **Catastrophe** means "conclusion."

67. **snuff:** literally, the burned wick-end, which should be removed so that the fresh wick may burn properly; an obstacle.

68. **apprehensive:** quick to grasp.

69-70. **whose judgments are /Mere fathers of their garments:** who devote their minds to planning their apparel.

So like a courtier, contempt nor bitterness
Were in his pride or sharpness; if they were,
His equal had awaked them; and his honor,
Clock to itself, knew the true minute when   45
Exception bid him speak, and at this time
His tongue obeyed his hand. Who were below him
He used as creatures of another place
And bowed his eminent top to their low ranks,
Making them proud of his humility   50
In their poor praise he humbled. Such a man
Might be a copy to these younger times;
Which, followed well, would demonstrate them now
But goers backward.

Ber.   His good remembrance, sir,   55
Lies richer in your thoughts than on his tomb;
So in approof lives not his epitaph
As in your royal speech.

King. Would I were with him! He would always
    say—   60
Methinks I hear him now; his plausive words
He scattered not in ears but grafted them
To grow there and to bear—"Let me not live"—
This his good melancholy oft began,
On the catastrophe and heel of pastime,   65
When it was out—"Let me not live," quoth he,
"After my flame lacks oil, to be the snuff
Of younger spirits, whose apprehensive senses
All but new things disdain; whose judgments are
Mere fathers of their garments; whose constancies   70
Expire before their fashions." This he wished:

**77. They that least lend it you shall lack you
first:** even those who think they do not love you will
miss you when you are gone; see also V. iii. 71.

78. fill a place: that is, merely take up room use-
lessly.

84. several: different; various.

██

I. iii. The Countess learns from her steward that
Helena loves Bertram. After determined questioning
she wrings from Helena a confession of her feelings
and discovers that Helena plans to go to Paris to
attempt the King's cure. Her father bequeathed to
her a miraculous remedy that might be successful.
Helena admits that she would probably not have
conceived the idea had Bertram not been at Paris.
The Countess is doubtful whether the girl can succeed where so many doctors have failed, but Helena's
optimism is so contagious that she gives permission
for the undertaking.

████████████████████████████████

3-4. even your content: please you; the word
even is a bookkeeper's term.

4. calendar: example; record.

I, after him, do after him wish too,
Since I nor wax nor honey can bring home,
I quickly were dissolved from my hive,
To give some laborers room.   75
    2. *Lo.*   You're loved, sir:
They that least lend it you shall lack you first.
    King. I fill a place, I know't. How long is't, Count,
Since the physician at your father's died?
He was much famed.   80
    Ber.   Some six months since, my lord.
    King. If he were living, I would try him yet—
Lend me an arm—the rest have worn me out
With several applications; nature and sickness
Debate it at their leisure. Welcome, Count;   85
My son's no dearer.
    Ber.   Thank your Majesty.
                              Exeunt. Flourish.

[Scene III. Rossillion. The Count's palace.]

*Enter Countess, [Rinaldo, the] Steward, and
        [Lavatch, the], Clown.*

    Coun. I will now hear. What say you of this gen-
tlewoman?
    Rin. Madam, the care I have had to even your con-
tent I wish might be found in the calendar of my
past endeavors; for then we wound our modesty and   5

6. **clearness:** integrity; purity.
18. **go to the world:** marry.
23-4. **Service is no heritage:** proverbial; **heritage** means "inheritance."
26. **barnes:** children; another proverbial idea.

make foul the clearness of our deservings when of ourselves we publish them.

Coun. What does this knave here? Get you gone, sirrah. The complaints I have heard of you I do not all believe: 'tis my slowness that I do not; for I know   10 you lack not folly to commit them and have ability enough to make such knaveries yours.

Lav. 'Tis not unknown to you, madam, I am a poor fellow.

Coun. Well, sir.   15

Lav. No, madam, 'tis not so well that I am poor, though many of the rich are damned; but, if I may have your Ladyship's good will to go to the world, Isbel the woman and I will do as we may.

Coun. Wilt thou needs be a beggar?   20

Lav. I do beg your good will in this case.

Coun. In what case?

Lav. In Isbel's case and mine own. Service is no heritage; and I think I shall never have the blessing of God till I have issue o' my body; for they say   25 barnes are blessings.

Coun. Tell me thy reason why thou wilt marry.

Lav. My poor body, madam, requires it. I am driven on by the flesh; and he must needs go that the Dovil drives.   30

Coun. Is this all your Worship's reason?

Lav. Faith, madam, I have other holy reasons, such as they are.

Coun. May the world know them?

Lav. I have been, madam, a wicked creature, as   35

37. **repent:** i.e., "at leisure," according to another proverb.

42. **shallow . . . in:** ignorant in the matter of.

44. **ears:** plows.

45. **gives me leave to in the crop:** allows me time to gather the crop; **cuckold:** the standard term for a man whose wife is unfaithful.

49. **ergo:** therefore.

51. **what they are:** i.e., cuckolds all.

52. **Charbon:** a corruption of the French *chair bonne* (good flesh); Puritans did not believe in fasting.

53. **Poysam:** *poisson*, French for "fish."

55. **jowl:** knock. Cuckolds were said to have horns.

59. **next:** nearest.

62. **marriage comes by destiny:** proverbial; compare "Marriages are made in Heaven."

63. **by kind:** i.e., because it is natural for it to do so. **Cuckoo** is an alternate form of "cuckold"; Lavatch implies that cuckoldom is as inevitable as marriage.

you and all flesh and blood are; and, indeed, I do
marry that I may repent.

Coun. Thy marriage, sooner than thy wickedness.

Lav. I am out o' friends, madam; and I hope to
have friends for my wife's sake.   40

Coun. Such friends are thine enemies, knave.

Lav. Y'are shallow, madam, in great friends; for
the knaves come to do that for me which I am
aweary of. He that ears my land spares my team and
gives me leave to in the crop. If I be his cuckold, he's   45
my drudge. He that comforts my wife is the cher-
isher of my flesh and blood; he that cherishes my
flesh and blood loves my flesh and blood; he that
loves my flesh and blood is my friend: ergo, he that
kisses my wife is my friend. If men could be con-   50
tented to be what they are, there were no fear in
marriage; for young Charbon the Puritan and old
Poysam the papist, howsome'er their hearts are sev-
ered in religion, their heads are both one; they may
jowl horns together like any deer i' the herd.   55

Coun. Wilt thou ever be a foul-mouthed and ca-
lumnious knave?

Lav. A prophet I, madam; and I speak the truth
the next way:

> For I the ballad will repeat,   60
> Which men full true shall find;
> Your marriage comes by destiny,
> Your cuckoo sings by kind.

Coun. Get you gone, sir; I'll talk with you more
anon.   65

72. Fond: foolishly. The *she* of the song is probably King Priam's wife, Hecuba.

73. King Priam's joy: his son, Paris, who abducted Helen and thus caused the Trojan War.

80-1. corrupt the song: the song possibly spoke of one bad among nine good, referring to the sons of Priam.

82-3. a purifying o' the song: i.e., in designating as good one woman in ten, when the clown feels that the proportion of good women to bad is not really that high.

85. tithe-woman: the one good woman in ten. The word is formed by analogy with "tithe-pig," the parson's due from a parishioner.

86. quotha: says she; **And:** if.

88. mend the lottery: improve the odds.

89. 'a: he.

93. honesty: chastity.

94-5. wear the surplice of humility over the black gown of a big heart: i.e., wear the surplice decreed by the Church, which was repugnant to the Puritans, over the Puritan's black gown, concealing the resentment he felt at being compelled to conform in appearance.

Rin. May it please you, madam, that he bid Helen
come to you: of her I am to speak.

Coun. Sirrah, tell my gentlewoman I would speak
with her; Helen I mean.

Lav. "Was this fair face the cause," quoth she,   70
     "Why the Grecians sacked Troy?
   Fond done, done fond,
     Was this King Priam's joy?"
  With that she sighed as she stood,
  With that she sighed as she stood,   75
   And gave this sentence then;
 "Among nine bad if one be good,
 Among nine bad if one be good,
   There's yet one good in ten."

Coun. What, one good in ten? You corrupt the   80
song, sirrah.

Lav. One good woman in ten, madam; which is a
purifying o' the song. Would God would serve the
world so all the year! We'd find no fault with the
tithe-woman, if I were the parson. One in ten,   85
quotha! And we might have a good woman born but
or every blazing star, or at an earthquake, 'twould
mend the lottery well. A man may draw his heart
out ere 'a pluck one.

Coun. You'll be gone, sir knave, and do as I com-   90
mand you!

Lav. That man should be at woman's command,
and yet no hurt done! Though honesty be no Puritan, yet it will do no hurt; it will wear the surplice
of humility over the black gown of a big heart. I am   95

96. **forsooth:** indeed.

103. **make title to:** claim.

106. **late:** lately.

109-10. **touched not any stranger sense:** were unheard by any other than herself.

115. **her poor knight surprised:** i.e., the virgin Helena conquered.

117. **touch:** tone.

119. **sithence:** since.

125. **misdoubt:** doubt.

going, forsooth; the business is for Helen to come
hither.   *Exit.*

Coun. Well, now.

Rin. I know, madam, you love your gentlewoman
entirely.   100

Coun. Faith, I do: her father bequeathed her to
me; and she herself, without other advantage, may
lawfully make title to as much love as she finds.
There is more owing her than is paid; and more shall
be paid her than she'll demand.   105

Rin. Madam, I was very late more near her than
I think she wished me. Alone she was and did com-
municate to herself her own words to her own ears;
she thought, I dare vow for her, they touched not
any stranger sense. Her matter was, she loved your   110
son. Fortune, she said, was no goddess, that had put
such difference betwixt their two estates; Love, no
god, that would not extend his might only where
qualities were level; Dian, no queen of virgins, that
would suffer her poor knight surprised, without res- 115
cue in the first assault or ransom afterward. This
she delivered in the most bitter touch of sorrow that
e'er I heard virgin exclaim in, which I held my duty
speedily to acquaint you withal, sithence, in the loss
that may happen, it concerns you something to know   120
it.

Coun. You have discharged this honestly; keep it
to yourself. Many likelihoods informed me of this
before, which hung so tott'ring in the balance that I
could neither believe nor misdoubt. Pray you, leave   125

129. **If ever we are Nature's, these are ours:** i.e., these emotional pangs afflict every human.

131. **Our blood to us, this to our blood is born:** this passion is as natural to us as the blood in our veins.

132. **show and seal:** certified evidence.

134. **our:** i.e., her own.

136. **on't:** of (as a result of) it.

151. **curd:** curdle.

me. Stall this in your bosom; and I thank you for
your honest care. I will speak with you further anon.

Exit [Rinaldo].

Enter Helena.

Even so it was with me when I was young.
  If ever we are Nature's, these are ours; this thorn
Doth to our rose of youth rightly belong;   130
  Our blood to us, this to our blood is born.
It is the show and seal of Nature's truth,
Where love's strong passion is impressed in youth.
By our remembrances of days foregone,
Such were our faults; or then we thought them none. 135
Her eye is sick on't; I observe her now.

  Hel. What is your pleasure, madam?

  Coun.   You know, Helen,
I am a mother to you.

  Hel. Mine honorable mistress.   140

  Coun.   Nay, a mother:
Why not a mother? When I said "a mother,"
Methought you saw a serpent. What's in "mother,"
That you start at it? I say, I am your mother,
And put you in the catalogue of those   145
That were enwombed mine. 'Tis often seen,
Adoption strives with nature; and choice breeds
A native slip to us from foreign seeds.
You ne'er oppressed me with a mother's groan,
Yet I express to you a mother's care.   150
God's mercy, maiden! does it curd thy blood

153. **distempered:** disturbed.

154. **Iris:** rainbow; **rounds thine eye:** i.e., circles her eye with the moisture of tears.

161. **note:** distinction.

170. **Can't no other:** can it not be otherwise.

178. **head:** source; **gross:** obvious.

To say I am thy mother? What's the matter,
That this distempered messenger of wet,
The many-colored Iris, rounds thine eye?
Why? that you are my daughter?   155

  Hel.   That I am not.

  Coun. I say I am your mother.

  Hel.   Pardon, madam;
The Count Rossillion cannot be my brother:
I am from humble, he from honored name;   160
No note upon my parents, his all noble.
My master, my dear lord, he is; and I
His servant live and will his vassal die.
He must not be my brother.

  Coun.   Nor I your mother?   165

  Hel. You are my mother, madam; would you were—
So that my lord your son were not my brother—
Indeed my mother! or were you both our mothers,
I care no more for than I do for Heaven,
So I were not his sister. Can't no other,   170
But, I your daughter, he must be my brother?

  Coun. Yes, Helen, you might be my daughter-in-
    law.
God shield you mean it not! daughter and mother
So strive upon your pulse. What, pale again?   175
My fear hath catched your fondness. Now I see
The myst'ry of your loneliness and find
Your salt tears' head. Now to all sense 'tis gross
You love my son; invention is ashamed,
Against the proclamation of thy passion,   180
To say thou dost not. Therefore tell me true;

185. **in their kind:** after their fashion.

187. **That truth should be suspected:** so that truth must be guessed at for lack of frank revelation.

188. **wound a goodly clew:** hopelessly entangled yourself.

197. **Go not about:** do not be evasive; **a bond:** an obligation.

198. **Whereof the world takes note:** which the world accepts.

200. **appeached:** accused you.

Love and the "captious and intenible sieve." From Guillaume de la Perrière, *Le théâtre des bons engins* (1539).
(See line 212)

But tell me then, 'tis so; for, look, thy cheeks
Confess it, the one to the other; and thine eyes
See it so grossly shown in thy behaviors
That in their kind they speak it: only sin   185
And hellish obstinacy tie thy tongue,
That truth should be suspected. Speak, is't so?
If it be so, you have wound a goodly clew;
If it be not, forswear't. Howe'er, I charge thee,
As Heaven shall work in me for thine avail,   190
To tell me truly.

    Hel.   Good madam, pardon me!

    Coun. Do you love my son?

    Hel.   Your pardon, noble mistress!

    Coun. Love you my son?   195

    Hel.   Do not you love him, madam?

    Coun. Go not about; my love hath in't a bond,
Whereof the world takes note. Come, come, disclose
The state of your affection; for your passions
Have to the full appeached.   200

    Hel.   Then, I confess,
Here on my knee, before high Heaven and you,
That before you, and next unto high Heaven,
I love your son.

My friends were poor but honest; so's my love.   205
Be not offended, for it hurts not him
That he is loved of me. I follow him not
By any token of presumptuous suit;
Nor would I have him till I do deserve him;
Yet never know how that desert should be.   210
I know I love in vain, strive against hope,

212. **captious and intenible sieve:** hope is likened to a sieve, which readily receives but is incapable of holding. The sieve's capacity is infinite, since it does not retain what is put into it.

214. **lack not to lose still:** have enough hope to continue thus losing it forever.

218. **encounter:** quarrel.

220. **Whose aged honor cites:** whose honorable old age proves.

222-23. **that your Dian /Was both herself and Love:** so that your love could be chaste as well as passionate.

226. **find that:** find that which.

227. **riddle-like:** like a Sphinx, never revealing her secret.

236. **For general sovereignty:** because of their general efficacy.

238-39. **whose faculties inclusive were /More than they were in note:** whose power was greater than was known; i.e., her father advised caution in using these powerful prescriptions.

240. **approved:** of demonstrated potency.

Yet, in this captious and intenible sieve,
I still pour in the waters of my love
And lack not to lose still. Thus, Indian-like,
Religious in mine error, I adore   215
The sun, that looks upon his worshiper
But knows of him no more. My dearest madam,
Let not your hate encounter with my love
For loving where you do: but if yourself,
Whose aged honor cites a virtuous youth,   220
Did ever in so true a flame of liking
Wish chastely and love dearly, that your Dian
Was both herself and Love; O, then, give pity
To her whose state is such that cannot choose
But lend and give where she is sure to lose;   225
That seeks not to find that her search implies,
But riddle-like lives sweetly where she dies!
   Coun. Had you not lately an intent—speak truly—
To go to Paris?
   Hel.   Madam, I had.   230
   Coun.   Wherefore? tell true.
   Hel. I will tell truth; by Grace itself I swear.
You know my father left me some prescriptions
Of rare and proved effects, such as his reading
And manifest experience had collected   235
For general sovereignty; and that he willed me
In heedfullest reservation to bestow them,
As notes whose faculties inclusive were
More than they were in note. Amongst the rest
There is a remedy approved set down,   240
To cure the desperate languishings whereof

247. **conversation:** occupation.

248. **Haply:** perhaps.

250. **tender:** offer.

255. **Emboweled:** disemboweled. Possibly a reference to the disemboweling of traitors, some of whom were Catholics whose doctrine differed from that of the established church. The sense is that the profoundest depths of the doctors' knowledge had been exhausted.

255-56. **left off /The danger to itself:** left the dangerous ailment to run its course.

259. **that:** so that.

264. **well-lost:** i.e., well worth losing in such an effort.

268-69. **leave and love:** loving permission to go.

The King is rendered lost.
  Coun.   This was your motive
For Paris, was it? speak.
  Hel. My lord your son made me to think of this;   245
Else Paris, and the medicine, and the King,
Had from the conversation of my thoughts
Haply been absent then.
  Coun.   But think you, Helen,
If you should tender your supposed aid,   250
He would receive it? He and his physicians
Are of a mind: he, that they cannot help him;
They, that they cannot help. How shall they credit
A poor unlearned virgin, when the schools,
Emboweled of their doctrine, have left off   255
The danger to itself?
  Hel.   There's something in't
More than my father's skill, which was the great'st
Of his profession, that his good receipt
Shall for my legacy be sanctified   260
By the luckiest stars in Heaven: and, would your Honor
But give me leave to try success, I'd venture
The well-lost life of mine on His Grace's cure
By such a day and hour.   265
  Coun.   Dost thou believe't?
  Hel. Ay, madam, knowingly.
  Coun. Why, Helen, thou shalt have my leave and love,
Means and attendants, and my loving greetings   270
To those of mine in court. I'll stay at home

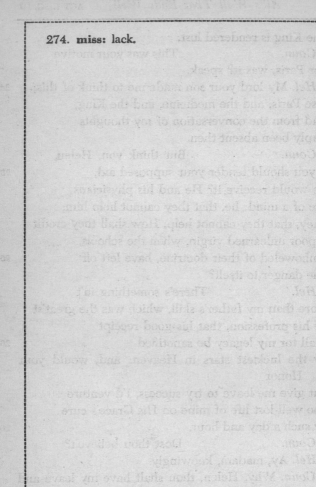

274. miss: lack.

And pray God's blessing into thy attempt.
Be gone tomorrow; and be sure of this,
What I can help thee to, thou shalt not miss.

Exeunt.

ALL'S WELL
THAT ENDS WELL

❦

ACT II

II. i. The young Frenchmen depart for the Italian wars. Bertram is resentful at being kept at court because he is too young, and Parolles advises him to steal away without the King's permission. In the meantime, Lord Lafew announces the arrival of Helena and her proposal to attempt the King's cure. He speaks so highly of Helena that the King agrees to receive her. Helena promises to cure the King within twenty-four hours on pain of disgrace, torture, and death if she fails. If she is successful, she asks only that the King grant her the husband of her choice. The King at length is persuaded by her earnest eloquence and agrees to the bargain.

4. both: the King is apparently addressing two groups of lords: one group is bound to fight with the Florentines, the other with the Sienese, having received the King's permission in I. ii.

8. After well-entered soldiers: after making a good beginning as soldiers.

11. owes: possesses.

15. bated: excepted. The King means to exclude from the adjective **higher** those associated with **the fall of the last monarchy,** an allusion of uncertain meaning. The Florentine/Sienese conflict derives from Boccaccio's original tale, and it is probably useless to seek a precise historical reference in Shakespeare's words.

17-8. when /The bravest questant shrinks, find what you seek: i.e., never give up the pursuit of your quarry, honor. The metaphor may be from hunting, the lords being compared with hounds on the trail.

23

ACT II

[Scene I. Paris. The King's palace.]

Flourish cornets. Enter the King, [attended] with divers young Lords, taking leave for the Florentine war; [Bertram,] and Parolles.

King. Farewell, young lords; these warlike principles
Do not throw from you: and you, my lords, farewell.
Share the advice betwixt you; if both gain, all
The gift doth stretch itself as 'tis received   5
And is enough for both.
    1. Lo.   'Tis our hope, sir,
After well-entered soldiers, to return
And find your Grace in health.
    King. No, no, it cannot be; and yet my heart   10
Will not confess he owes the malady
That doth my life besiege. Farewell, young lords.
Whether I live or die, be you the sons
Of worthy Frenchmen: let higher Italy—
Those bated that inherit but the fall   15
Of the last monarchy—see that you come
Not to woo honor but to wed it: when
The bravest questant shrinks, find what you seek,

23

19. **cry you loud:** loudly trumpet your praises.

30. **spark:** fiery gallant.

33. **kept a coil:** fussed over.

35. **And:** if.

37. **smock:** woman.

38. **Creaking my shoes on the plain masonry:** i.e., dancing attendance in courtly fashion.

39-40. **no sword worn /But one to dance with:** gentlemen wore light, ornamental swords at dances.

43. **accessary:** accomplice (in stealing away).

44-5. **our parting is a tortured body:** Bertram satirizes affected courtly speech in expressing the pain of saying good-by to the lord.

Fame. From Henry Peacham, *Minerva Britanna* (1618).

That Fame may cry you loud. I say farewell.

1. Lo. Health at your bidding serve your Majesty!   20

King. Those girls of Italy, take heed of them:
They say our French lack language to deny
If they demand. Beware of being captives
Before you serve.

Lords.   Our hearts receive your warnings.   25

King. Farewell. [*To Attendants*] Come hither to
    me.   [*Exit.*]

1. Lo. O my sweet lord, that you will stay behind
    us!

Par. 'Tis not his fault, the spark.   30

2. Lo.   O, 'tis brave wars!

Par. Most admirable: I have seen those wars.

Ber. I am commanded here, and kept a coil with
"Too young," and "the next year," and "'tis too early."

Par. And thy mind stand to't, boy, steal away   35
bravely.

Ber. I shall stay here the forehorse to a smock,
Creaking my shoes on the plain masonry,
Till honor be bought up and no sword worn
But one to dance with! By Heaven, I'll steal away.   40

1. Lo. There's honor in the theft.

Par.   Commit it, Count.

2. Lo. I am your accessary; and so, farewell.

Ber. I grow to you, and our parting is a tortured
body.   45

1. Lo. Farewell, captain.

2. Lo. Sweet Monsieur Parolles!

Par. Noble heroes, my sword and yours are kin.
Good sparks and lustrous, a word, good metals. You

52. **sinister: left; entrenched:** gashed.

59. **list:** confine.

61. **wear themselves in the cap of the time:** are the ornaments of the time, like the brooches and feathers that were worn in bonnets.

61-2. **there do muster true gait:** i.e., and in so doing show mastery of behavior befitting the time.

63. **most received:** most auspicious or popular.

64. **measure:** dance.

65. **dilated:** expanded.

shall find in the regiment of the Spinii one Captain 50
Spurio, with his cicatrice, an emblem of war, here on
his sinister cheek. It was this very sword entrenched
it. Say to him, I live; and observe his reports for me.

1. Lo. We shall, noble captain.   [*Exeunt Lords.*]

Par. Mars dote on you for his novices! What will 55
ye do?

Ber. Stay: the King.

Enter King.

Par. Use a more spacious ceremony to the noble
lords. You have restrained yourself within the list of
too cold an adieu. Be more expressive to them; for 60
they wear themselves in the cap of the time, there do
muster true gait, eat, speak, and move under the influence of the most received star; and, though the
Devil lead the measure, such are to be followed.
After them, and take a more dilated farewell. 65

Ber. And I will do so.

Par. Worthy fellows; and like to prove most sinewy
swordmen.   *Exeunt [Bertram and Parolles].*

Enter Lafew.

Lafew. [*Kneeling*] Pardon, my lord, for me and for
my tidings. 70

King. I'll fee thee to stand up.

Lafew. Then here's a man stands that has brought
his pardon.

I would you had kneeled, my lord, to ask me mercy
And that at my bidding you could so stand up. 75

76. **so:** provided that; **pate:** head.

78. **Good faith, across:** "yes, indeed, I would be content that you had broken my head across, if only you were able to stand."

82. **eat no grapes:** referring to the Aesop fable of the fox, who, failing to reach a tempting cluster of grapes, declared that they were sour anyway.

83. **and if:** if.

84-5. **medicine:** doctor.

87. **Quicken:** animate; **canary:** a lively dance.

89. **King Pepin:** a Frankish king of the eighth century, therefore one a very long time dead.

98. **profession:** what she claims she can perform.

99-100. **more /Than I dare blame my weakness:** to a greater degree than can be explained by the susceptibility of a man of my age.

104. **admiration:** marvel; prodigy.

105. **take off:** imitate derisively.

The fox and the grapes. From Aesop, *Fabulae* (1590).

King. I would I had; so I had broke thy pate
And asked thee mercy for't.

   Lafew. Good faith, across: but, my good lord, 'tis
     thus:
Will you be cured of your infirmity?   80

   King. No.

   Lafew. O, will you eat no grapes, my royal fox?
Yes, but you will my noble grapes, and if
My royal fox could reach them. I have seen a medi-
     cine   85
That's able to breathe life into a stone,
Quicken a rock, and make you dance canary
With sprightly fire and motion; whose simple touch
Is powerful to araise King Pepin, nay,
To give great Charlemain a pen in's hand,   90
And write to her a love line.

   King.   What "her" is this?

   Lafew. Why, Doctor She. My lord, there's one ar-
     rived,
If you will see her. Now, by my faith and honor,   95
If seriously I may convey my thoughts
In this my light deliverance, I have spoke
With one that in her sex, her years, profession,
Wisdom, and constancy hath amazed me more
Than I dare blame my weakness. Will you see her, 100
For that is her demand, and know her business?
That done, laugh well at me.

   King.   Now, good Lafew.
Bring in the admiration, that we with thee
May spend our wonder too, or take off thine   105
By wond'ring how thou tookst it.

107. **fit:** satisfy.

115. **Cressid's uncle:** Pandarus, the original pander or pimp.

117. **follow:** concern.

120. **well found:** acknowledged an expert.

126. **of his old experience the only darling:** the most treasured remedy known to him from his long practice.

127. **triple:** third.

132. **appliance:** application.

Lafew.   Nay, I'll fit you,
And not be all day neither.   [*Exit.*]
King. Thus he his special nothing ever prologues.

Enter [Lafew, with] Helena.

Lafew. Nay, come your ways.   110
King.   This haste hath wings indeed.
Lafew. Nay, come your ways;
This is His Majesty, say your mind to him.
A traitor you do look like; but such traitors
His Majesty seldom fears. I am Cressid's uncle,   115
That dare leave two together: fare you well.   *Exit.*
King. Now, fair one, does your business follow us?
Hel. Ay, my good lord.
Gerard de Narbon was my father;
In what he did profess, well found.   120
King.   I knew him.
Hel. The rather will I spare my praises towards him;
Knowing him is enough. On's bed of death
Many receipts he gave me; chiefly one,
Which, as the dearest issue of his practice   125
And of his old experience the only darling,
He bade me store up, as a triple eye,
Safer than mine own two, more dear. I have so;
And, hearing your high Majesty is touched
With that malignant cause wherein the honor   130
Of my dear father's gift stands chief in power,
I come to tender it and my appliance,
With all bound humbleness.
King.   We thank you, maidon,

137. **The congregated college:** in Shakespeare's England this would have been the assembled members of the College of Physicians.

141. **prostitute:** submit shamefully.

142. **empirics:** quacks, or their remedies.

142-43. **dissever so /Our great self and our credit:** so disgrace myself.

144. **senseless help:** nonsensical cure; **when help past sense we deem:** when a cure seems to me beyond reasonable expectation.

145. **my duty:** consciousness of having done my duty.

146. **enforce:** urge.

148. **A modest one:** i.e., a charitable view of her motives.

155. **set up your rest:** are resolved.

157. **minister:** agent.

But may not be so credulous of cure,   135
When our most learned doctors leave us, and
The congregated college have concluded
That laboring art can never ransom nature
From her inaidable estate. I say we must not
So stain our judgment, or corrupt our hope,   140
To prostitute our past-cure malady
To empirics, or to dissever so
Our great self and our credit, to esteem
A senseless help, when help past sense we deem.

  Hel. My duty, then, shall pay me for my pains.   145
I will no more enforce mine office on you;
Humbly entreating from your royal thoughts
A modest one, to bear me back again.

  King. I cannot give thee less, to be called grateful.
Thou thoughtst to help me, and such thanks I give 150
As one near death to those that wish him live.
But what at full I know thou knowst no part;
I knowing all my peril, thou no art.

  Hel. What I can do can do no hurt to try,
Since you set up your rest 'gainst remedy.   155
He that of greatest works is finisher,
Oft does them by the weakest minister.
So Holy Writ in babes hath judgment shown,
When judges have been babes; great floods have
    flown   160
From simple sources; and great seas have dried,
When miracles have by the great'st been denied.
Oft expectation fails, and most oft there
Where most it promises; and oft it hits
Where hope is coldest and despair most fits.   165

170. **Inspired merit so by breath is barred:** thus assistance divinely inspired is denied.

172. **square our guess by shows:** judge by outward appearances.

177-78. **proclaim /Myself against the level of mine aim:** boast beyond my power to perform.

184-85. **bring /Their fiery torcher his diurnal ring:** transport the sun-god on his daily circuit.

187. **Hesperus:** another name for the evening star (Venus).

188. **pilot's glass:** nautical hourglass.

190. **sound:** i.e., restored to sound condition.

194. **Tax:** charge; **impudence:** shamelessness.

The chariot of the sun. From Claude Menestrier, *L'art des emblèmes* (1684).

King. I must not hear thee. Fare thee well, kind
    maid:
Thy pains not used must by thyself be paid:
Proffers not took reap thanks for their reward.
    Hel. Inspired merit so by breath is barred.   170
It is not so with Him that all things knows,
As 'tis with us that square our guess by shows;
But most it is presumption in us when
The help of Heaven we count the act of men.
Dear sir, to my endeavors give consent;   175
Of Heaven, not me, make an experiment.
I am not an impostor that proclaim
Myself against the level of mine aim;
But know I think, and think I know most sure,
My art is not past power nor you past cure.   180
    King. Art thou so confident? Within what space
Hopest thou my cure?
    Hel.   The great'st Grace lending grace,
Ere twice the horses of the sun shall bring
Their fiery torcher his diurnal ring;   185
Ere twice in murk and occidental damp
Moist Hesperus hath quenched her sleepy lamp;
Or four-and-twenty times the pilot's glass
Hath told the thievish minutes how they pass;
What is infirm from your sound parts shall fly,   190
Health shall live free and sickness freely die.
    King. Upon thy certainty and confidence
What darest thou venture?
    Hel.   Tax of impudence,
A strumpet's boldness, a divulged shame   195
Traduced by odious ballads; my maiden's name

197. **ne worse of worst extended:** nor will it be a worse punishment (than the disgrace already described) if.

202-3. **what impossibility would slay /In common sense, sense saves another way:** what common sense dismisses as impossible, another sense (intuition?) accepts.

205. **estimate:** value.

207. **happiness and prime:** i.e., one in the fortunate prime of life.

208. **Thou this to hazard:** for you to hazard this.

212. **break time:** fail to meet the promised deadline; **property:** precise condition.

217. **make it even:** fulfill it.

224. **image:** counterpart.

Seared; otherwise, ne worse of worst extended,
With vilest torture let my life be ended.

  King. Methinks in thee some blessed spirit doth
    speak   200
His powerful sound within an organ weak;
And what impossibility would slay
In common sense, sense saves another way.
Thy life is dear, for all that life can rate
Worth name of life in thee hath estimate: 205
Youth, beauty, wisdom, courage, all
That happiness and prime can happy call.
Thou this to hazard needs must intimate
Skill infinite or monstrous desperate.
Sweet practicer, thy physic I will try,   210
That ministers thine own death if I die.

  Hel. If I break time, or flinch in property
Of what I spoke, unpitied let me die,
And well deserved. Not helping, death's my fee;
But, if I help, what do you promise me?   215

  King. Make thy demand.

  Hel.   But will you make it even?

  King. Ay, by my scepter and my hopes of Heaven.

  Hel. Then shalt thou give me with thy kingly hand
What husband in thy power I will command.   220
Exempted be from me the arrogance
To choose from forth the royal blood of France,
My low and humble name to propagate
With any branch or image of thy state;
But such a one, thy vassal, whom I know   225
Is free for me to ask, thee to bestow.

  King. Here is my hand; the premises observed,

230. **still:** ever; in everything.

235-36. **proceed /As high as word:** perform thy promise.

⸺⸺⸺⸺⸺⸺⸺⸺⸺⸺⸺⸺⸺

II. ii. At Rossillion, the Countess prepares her clown, Lavatch, for an errand to deliver a letter to Helena at the French court.

⸺⸺⸺⸺⸺⸺⸺⸺

1-2, **put you to the height of your breeding:** try your manners to the utmost.

3. **highly fed and lowly taught:** echoing the proverb "Better fed than taught."

6. **put off:** brush aside.

9. **put it off:** get rid of it.

10. **leg:** low bow.

Thy will by my performance shall be served:
So make the choice of thy own time, for I,
Thy resolved patient, on thee still rely.   230
More should I question thee, and more I must,
Though more to know could not be more to trust,
From whence thou camest, how tended on; but rest
Unquestioned welcome and undoubted blest.
Give me some help here, ho! If thou proceed   235
As high as word, my deed shall match thy deed.

Flourish. Exeunt.

[Scene II. Rossillion. The Count's palace.]

Enter Countess and [Lavatch, the] Clown.

Coun. Come on, sir; I shall now put you to the
height of your breeding.

Lav. I will show myself highly fed and lowly taught.
I know my business is but to the court.

Coun. To the court! why, what place make you   5
special, when you put off that with such contempt?
"But to the court"!

Lav. Truly, madam, if God have lent a man any
manners, he may easily put it off at court: he that cannot make a leg, put off's cap, kiss his hand, and say   10
nothing, has neither leg, hands, lip, nor cap; and, indeed, such a fellow, to say precisely, were not for the
court. But for me, I have an answer will serve all men.

17. **quatch:** not found elsewhere; perhaps akin to "quash" or "squat," i.e., flat.

20. **ten groats:** the usual attorney's fee, worth 3*s*. 4*d*., since a groat was worth fourpence.

21. **French crown:** both a familiar coin and a euphemism for a bald head caused by venereal (French) disease; **taffeta punk:** showy prostitute.

22. **Tib's rush:** a ring made of rushes, given by country wenches to their swains. **Tib** was a common name for a country girl.

25. **quean:** strumpet.

25-26. **as the nun's lip to the friar's mouth, nay, as the pudding to his skin:** see the proverb "As fit as a pudding for a friar's mouth." **Pudding** means "sausage."

38. **question:** conversation.

40. **O Lord, sir:** a meaningless phrase of affected courtiers.

Coun. Marry, that's a bountiful answer that fits all
questions.   15

Lav. It is like a barber's chair, that fits all buttocks,
the pin-buttock, the quatch-buttock, the brawn-but-
tock, or any buttock.

Coun. Will your answer serve to fit all questions?

Lav. As fit as ten groats is for the hand of an attor-   20
ney, as your French crown for your taffeta punk, as
Tib's rush for Tom's forefinger, as a pancake for
Shrove Tuesday, a morris for May Day, as the nail
to his hole, the cuckold to his horn, as a scolding
quean to a wrangling knave, as the nun's lip to the   25
friar's mouth, nay, as the pudding to his skin.

Coun. Have you, I say, an answer of such fitness
for all questions?

Lav. From below your duke to beneath your con-
stable, it will fit any question.   30

Coun. It must be an answer of most monstrous size
that must fit all demands.

Lav. But a trifle neither, in good faith, if the learned
should speak truth of it. Here it is, and all that be-
longs to't. Ask me if I am a courtier; it shall do you no   35
harm to learn.

Coun. To be young again, if we could! I will be a
fool in question, hoping to be the wiser by your answer. I pray you, sir, are you a courtier?

Lav. O Lord, sir! There's a simple putting-off.   40
More, more, a hundred of them.

Coun. Sir, I am a poor friend of yours that loves
you.

Lav. O Lord, sir! Thick, thick, spare not me.

47. **put me to't:** give me something more difficult to respond to.

53. **bound to't:** "bound over to answer" by a legal process and "bound to the whipping post."

57. **housewife:** hussy; wanton.

62. **present:** immediate.

63. **Commend me:** give my greetings.

69. **again:** back again.

Morris dancers. From a stained glass window.
(See line 23)

Coun. I think, sir, you can eat none of this homely   45
meat.

Lav. O Lord, sir! Nay, put me to't, I warrant you.

Coun. You were lately whipped, sir, as I think.

Lav. O Lord, sir! spare not me.

Coun. Do you cry, "O Lord, sir!" at your whipping,   50
and "spare not me"? Indeed your "O Lord, sir!" is
very sequent to your whipping; you would answer
very well to a whipping, if you were but bound to't.

Lav. I ne'er had worse luck in my life in my "O
Lord, sir!" I see things may serve long, but not serve   55
ever.

Coun. I play the noble housewife with the time,
To entertain it so merrily with a fool.

Lav. O Lord, sir! why, there't serves well again.

Coun. An end, sir; to your business. Give Helen   60
  this,
And urge her to a present answer back.
Commend me to my kinsmen and my son.
This is not much.

Lav. Not much commendation to them.   65

Coun. Not much employment for you: you understand me?

Lav. Most fruitfully: I am there before my legs.

Coun. Haste you again.

                              Exeunt.

II. iii. Helena's remedy has cured the King, and the court assembles so that she may claim the King's promise. When she selects Bertram, he at once scorns the idea of marrying a poor physician's daughter. The King tries to persuade him that she is noble in herself and that he will add honors and wealth to her natural endowments. When Bertram continues obstinate, the King reminds him that he must do as his guardian dictates. Bertram makes a pretense of yielding gracefully, but after the wedding Parolles encourages him to dismiss Helena on a pretext and abandon her for the wars.

<hr />

2. **modern:** commonplace.

3. **causeless:** proceeding of no known cause; unexplained.

4-5. **ensconcing ourselves into seeming knowledge:** taking refuge in apparent knowledge.

5-6. **submit ourselves to an unknown fear:** admit that there are forces we can neither understand nor control.

7. **argument:** subject.

10. **artists:** holders of arts degrees; learned doctors.

11. **Galen:** Greek physician and writer on medicine of the second century; **Paracelsus:** Theophrastus Bombastus von Hohenheim, Swiss physician and alchemist of the sixteenth century, who introduced many chemical remedies and disparaged the teachings of Greek medicine.

12. **authentic:** legally qualified.

(continued on next page)

[Scene III. Paris. The King's palace.]

Enter Count [Bertram], Lafew, and Parolles.

Lafew. They say miracles are past; and we have our philosophical persons, to make modern and familiar things supernatural and causeless. Hence is it that we make trifles of terrors; ensconcing ourselves into seeming knowledge, when we should submit ourselves to   5
an unknown fear.

Par. Why, 'tis the rarest argument of wonder that hath shot out in our latter times.

Ber. And so 'tis.

Lafew. To be relinquished of the artists—   10

Par. So I say: both of Galen and Paracelsus.

Lafew. Of all the learned and authentic fellows—

Par. Right! so I say.

Lafew. That gave him out incurable—

Par. Why, there 'tis; so say I too.   15

Lafew. Not to be helped—

Par. Right! as 'twere, a man assured of a—

Lafew. Uncertain life and sure death.

Par. Just, you say well; so would I have said.

Lafew. I may truly say, it is a novelty to the world.   20

Par. It is, indeed: if you will have it in showing, you shall read it in—what do ye call there?

Lafew. "A showing of a heavenly effect in an earthly actor."

14. **gave him out:** reported him.

19. **Just:** exactly.

21. **showing:** printed form.

23. **"A showing, etc.":** Lafew reads from a broadside relating the miraculous cure. In Elizabethan London such items of current news were frequently reported in ballads and broadsides.

Galen attending a patient. From Galen, *Opera* (1565). *(See line 11)*

26. **'fore me:** on my word.

29-30. **facinerious:** wicked.

34. **debile:** feeble.

41. **Lustig:** in a lusty state; hale and hearty.

43. **coranto:** lively dance.

44. **Mort du vinaigre:** literally, "death of vinegar," a meaningless oath.

48. **sense:** power of sensation; strength.

49. **repealed:** recalled; reinstated.

35

Par. That's it; I would have said the very same.   25

Lafew. Why, your dolphin is not lustier: 'fore me, I speak in respect—

Par. Nay, 'tis strange, 'tis very strange, that is the brief and the tedious of it, and he's of a most facinerious spirit that will not acknowledge it to be the—   30

Lafew. Very hand of Heaven.

Par. Ay, so I say.

Lafew. In a most weak—

Par. And debile minister, great power, great transcendence: which should, indeed, give us a further use   35
to be made than alone the recov'ry of the King, as to be—

Lafew. Generally thankful.

Enter King, Helena, and Attendants.

Par. I would have said it; you say well. Here comes the King.   40

Lafew. Lustig, as the Dutchman says: I'll like a maid the better, whilst I have a tooth in my head. Why, he's able to lead her a coranto.

Par. Mort du vinaigre! is not this Helen?

Lafew. 'Fore God, I think so.   45

King. Go, call before me all the lords in court.
                    [*Exit Attendant.*]
Sit, my preserver, by thy patient's side;
And with this healthful hand, whose banished sense
Thou hast repealed, a second time receive
The confirmation of my promised gift,   50
Which but attends thy naming.

51. **attends:** awaits.
52. **parcel:** group.
55. **Thy frank election make:** choose freely.
58. **Fall:** befall; **marry:** indeed.
59. **bay Curtal:** a docktailed bay horse.
60. **mouth:** i.e., teeth.
61. **writ:** claimed; possessed.
68. **simply:** absolutely; truly.
71. **be refused:** should you be refused.

Enter three or four Lords.

Fair maid, send forth thine eye: this youthful parcel
Of noble bachelors stand at my bestowing,
O'er whom both sovereign power and father's voice
I have to use. Thy frank election make;   55
Thou hast power to choose and they none to forsake.

  Hel. To each of you one fair and virtuous mistress
Fall, when Love please! marry, to each but one!

  Lafew. I'd give bay Curtal and his furniture
My mouth no more were broken than these boys',   60
And writ as little beard.

  King.   Peruse them well:
Not one of those but had a noble father.

  Hel. Gentlemen,
Heaven hath through me restored the King to health. 65

  All. We understand it and thank Heaven for you.

  Hel. I am a simple maid; and therein wealthiest
That I protest I simply am a maid.
Please it your Majesty, I have done already:
The blushes in my cheeks thus whisper me,   70
"We blush that thou shouldst choose; but, be refused,
Let the white death sit on thy cheek forever;
We'll ne'er come there again."

  King.   Make choice and see;
Who shuns thy love shuns all his love in me.   75

  Hel. Now, Dian, from thy altar do I fly;
And to imperial Love, that god most high,
Do my sighs stream.

                    She addresses her to a Lord.
                Sir, will you hear my suit?

83. **ames-ace:** two aces, the lowest throw at dice. Lafew is being ironic; he would like a chance to be Helena's husband.

101. **happy:** fortunate.

104-5. **thy father drunk wine:** i.e., you have a virile inheritance from your father.

1. Lo. And grant it.   80

Hel.   Thanks, sir; all the rest is mute.

Lafew. I had rather be in this choice than throw
ames-ace for my life.

Hel. The honor, sir, that flames in your fair eyes,
Before I speak, too threat'ningly replies.   85
Love make your fortunes twenty times above
Her that so wishes and her humble love!

2. Lo. No better, if you please.

Hel.   My wish receive,
Which great Love grant! and so I take my leave.   90

Lafew. Do all they deny her? And they were sons of
mine, I'd have them whipped; or I would send them
to the Turk, to make eunuchs of.

Hel. Be not afraid that I your hand should take;
I'll never do you wrong for your own sake.   95
Blessing upon your vows! and in your bed
Find fairer fortune, if you ever wed!

Lafew. These boys are boys of ice, they'll none have
her. Sure, they are bastards to the English; the French
ne'er got 'em.   100

Hel. You are too young, too happy, and too good,
To make yourself a son out of my blood.

4. Lo. Fair one, I think not so.

Lafew. There's one grape yet; I am sure thy father
drunk wine: but if thou beest not an ass, I am a youth 105
of fourteen; I have known thee already.

Hel. [To Bertram] I dare not say I take you; but I
   give
Me and my service, ever whilst I live,
Into your guiding power. This is the man.   110

124. **answer for:** repay.

125. **She had her breeding at my father's charge:** my father paid for her upbringing.

130. **Of:** of whatever.

131. **confound:** baffle.

131-32. **stands off /In differences so mighty:** i.e., Bertram's pride in his own blood sets him so apart in his own estimation.

138. **additions:** titles: **swell's:** swell us; **none:** not at all.

139. **dropsied:** unhealthy, in being unnaturally swollen.

139-40. **Good alone /Is good without a name:** goodness needs no title of honor to enhance it.

140. **vileness is so:** in like manner, vileness is no better for being called something else.

141. **property:** quality.

King. Why, then, young Bertram, take her; she's
   thy wife.

Ber. My wife, my liege! I shall beseech your Highness,

In such a business give me leave to use   115
The help of mine own eyes.

King.   Knowst thou not, Bertram,
What she has done for me?

Ber.   Yes, my good lord;
But never hope to know why I should marry her.   120

King. Thou knowst she has raised me from my
   sickly bed.

Ber. But follows it, my lord, to bring me down
Must answer for your raising? I know her well:
She had her breeding at my father's charge.   125
A poor physician's daughter my wife! Disdain
Rather corrupt me ever!

King. 'Tis only title thou disdainst in her, the which
I can build up. Strange is it that our bloods,
Of color, weight, and heat, poured all together,   130
Would quite confound distinction, yet stands off
In differences so mighty. If she be
All that is virtuous, save what thou dislikest,
A poor physician's daughter, thou dislikest
Of virtue for the name: but do not so.   135
From lowest place when virtuous things proceed,
The place is dignified by the doer's deed.
Where great additions swell's, and virtue none,
It is a dropsied honor. Good alone
Is good without a name; vileness is so.   140
The property by what it is should go,

143. **In these to Nature she's immediate heir:** i.e., these are natural endowments, not inherited by blood.

144-46. **That is honor's scorn /Which challenges itself as honor's born /And is not like the sire:** one who claims honor as his birthright is worthy only of scorn unless he justifies the claim by his honorable behavior.

149. **Deboshed:** debauched; i.e., debased by indiscriminate use.

154. **Virtue and she:** her virtuous self.

157-58. **Thou wrongst thyself, if thou shouldst strive to choose:** you are mistaken if you think yourself free to choose.

161. **My honor's at the stake; which to defeat:** my honor is being attacked, and to defeat the attack.

164. **misprision:** (1) misunderstanding; (2) false imprisonment.

164-65. **shackle up /My love and her desert:** i.e., treat with equal contempt my love and Helena's merit.

166. **poising us:** weighing myself; adding my own weight.

167. **weigh thee to the beam:** so outweigh you that your balance will strike the beam.

Not by the title. She is young, wise, fair;
In these to Nature she's immediate heir,
And these breed honor. That is honor's scorn
Which challenges itself as honor's born   145
And is not like the sire. Honors thrive
When rather from our acts we them derive
Than our foregoers. The mere word's a slave
Deboshed on every tomb, on every grave
A lying trophy, and as oft is dumb   150
Where dust and damned oblivion is the tomb
Of honored bones indeed. What should be said?
If thou canst like this creature as a maid,
I can create the rest. Virtue and she
Is her own dower; honor and wealth from me.   155
  Ber. I cannot love her, nor will strive to do't.
  King. Thou wrongst thyself, if thou shouldst strive
      to choose.
  Hel. That you are well restored, my lord, I'm glad:
Let the rest go.   160
  King. My honor's at the stake; which to defeat,
I must produce my power. Here, take her hand,
Proud scornful boy, unworthy this good gift;
That dost in vile misprision shackle up
My love and her desert; that canst not dream,   165
We, poising us in her defective scale,
Shall weigh thee to the beam; that wilt not know
It is in us to plant thine honor where
We please to have it grow. Check thy contempt!
Obey our will, which travails in thy good,   170
Believe not thy disdain, but presently

172. **obedient right:** right of obedience.

175. **staggers:** giddy conduct; **lapse:** slip.

178. **all terms:** any degree.

180. **fancy to your eyes:** inclination to your judgment.

188-89. **A counterpoise; if not to thy estate, /A balance more replete:** a dowry equaling if not surpassing thy estate.

193. **seem expedient on the now-born brief:** quickly follow the command I have just given.

194. **solemn:** ceremonial.

195. **more attend:** wait somewhat longer.

Do thine own fortunes that obedient right
Which both thy duty owes and our power claims;
Or I will throw thee from my care forever
Into the staggers and the careless lapse   175
Of youth and ignorance, both my revenge and hate
Loosing upon thee, in the name of justice,
Without all terms of pity. Speak! thine answer.

 Ber. Pardon, my gracious lord; for I submit
My fancy to your eyes. When I consider   180
What great creation and what dole of honor
Flies where you bid it, I find that she, which late
Was in my nobler thoughts most base, is now
The praised of the King; who, so ennobled,
Is as't were born so.   185

 King.   Take her by the hand
And tell her she is thine: to whom I promise
A counterpoise; if not to thy estate,
A balance more replete.

 Ber.   I take her hand.   190

 King. Good fortune and the favor of the King
Smile upon this contract; whose ceremony
Shall seem expedient on the now-born brief
And be performed tonight. The solemn feast
Shall more attend upon the coming space,   195
Expecting absent friends. As thou lovest her,
Thy love's to me religious; else, does err.

    Exeunt. Parolles and Lafew stay behind,
      commenting of this wedding.

 Lafew. Do you hear, monsieur? a word with you.
 Par. Your pleasure, sir?

205. **succeeding:** outcome; consequence.

207. **to what is man:** i.e., Parolles considers himself the equal of anyone.

208. **count's man:** count's servant.

212. **write "man":** call myself a man.

214. **What I dare too well do, I dare not do:** i.e., although I am man enough to deal with you, conscience forbids that I so treat an old man.

215. **two ordinaries:** the duration of two meals.

216-17. **make tolerable vent of thy travel:** tell your traveler's tales tolerably well.

217-19. **the scarves and the bannerets about thee did manifoldly dissuade me from believing thee a vessel of too great a burden:** i.e., you wear so many scarves and little banners (in addition to the scarf customarily worn by soldiers) that you look like a pleasure craft (frivolous fellow).

220. **found thee:** taken thy measure. Lafew refers to the proverb "Better lost than found."

221. **taking up:** challenging; contradicting.

227. **window of lattice:** i.e., transparency. Alehouses often had lattice windows, which adds to the insult.

Lafew. Your lord and master did well to make his 200
recantation.

Par. Recantation! My lord! my master!

Lafew. Ay; is it not a language I speak?

Par. A most harsh one, and not to be understood
without bloody succeeding. My master! 205

Lafew. Are you companion to the Count Rossillion?

Par. To any count, to all counts, to what is man.

Lafew. To what is count's man: count's master is of
another style.

Par. You are too old, sir; let it satisfy you; you are 210
too old.

Lafew. I must tell thee, sirrah, I write "man": to
which title age cannot bring thee.

Par. What I dare too well do, I dare not do.

Lafew. I did think thee, for two ordinaries, to be a 215
pretty wise fellow; thou didst make tolerable vent of
thy travel: it might pass. Yet the scarves and the bannerets about thee did manifoldly dissuade me from
believing thee a vessel of too great a burden. I have
now found thee; when I lose thee again, I care not. 220
Yet art thou good for nothing but taking up, and that
thou'rt scarce worth.

Par. Hadst thou not the privilege of antiquity upon
thee—

Lafew. Do not plunge thyself too far in anger, lest 225
thou hasten thy trial; which if—Lord have mercy on
thee for a hen! So, my good window of lattice, fare
thee well Thy casement I need not open, for I look
through thee. Give me thy hand.

235. **bate thee:** moderate my charge against thee; **scruple:** iota; mite.

240. **bondage:** i.e., of the scarves, which he wears as a matter of pride.

241-42. **or rather my knowledge, that I may say in the default, "He is a man I know":** or, better still, my full knowledge of your character, without having to associate with you, so that I can report you aright when your name is mentioned.

246-47. **as I will by thee:** that is, pass by thee.

Par. My lord, you give me most egregious indignity. 230

Lafew. Ay, with all my heart, and thou art worthy
of it.

Par. I have not, my lord, deserved it.

Lafew. Yes, good faith, ev'ry dram of it, and I will
not bate thee a scruple.   235

Par. Well, I shall be wiser.

Lafew. Ev'n as soon as thou canst, for thou hast to
pull at a smack o' the contrary. If ever thou beest
bound in thy scarf and beaten, thou shalt find what it
is to be proud of thy bondage. I have a desire to hold 240
my acquaintance with thee, or rather my knowledge,
that I may say in the default, "He is a man I know."

Par. My lord, you do me most insupportable vexa-
tion.

Lafew. I would it were hell pains for thy sake, and 245
my poor doing eternal: for doing I am past; as I will
by thee, in what motion age will give me leave. *Exit.*

Par. Well, thou hast a son shall take this disgrace
off me; scurvy, old, filthy, scurvy lord! Well, I must be
patient; there is no fettering of authority. I'll beat 250
him, by my life, if I can meet him with any convenience, and he were double and double a lord. I'll
have no more pity of his age than I would have of—I'll
beat him, and if I could but meet him again.

Enter Lafew.

Lafew. Sirrah, your lord and master's married. 255
There's news for you: you have a new mistress.

Par. I most unfeignedly beseech your Lordship to

258. make some reservation of your wrongs: be somewhat less insulting. Parolles objects to being called the servant of Bertram.

269. breathe: exercise.

271-72. picking a kernel out of a pomegranate: i.e., petty theft.

275. heraldry: the coat of arms signifying gentry, therefore, right of equality with those whom he treats familiarly.

A French soldier, scarved and plumed. From Jacob de Gheyn, *Maniement d'armes* (1608).
(See line 217)

make some reservation of your wrongs. He is my good
lord: Whom I serve above is my master.

Lafew. Who? God?   260

Par. Ay, sir.

Lafew. The Devil it is that's thy master. Why dost
thou garter up thy arms o' this fashion? Dost make
hose of thy sleeves? Do other servants so? Thou wert
best set thy lower part where thy nose stands. By   265
mine honor, if I were but two hours younger, I'd beat
thee. Methinkst thou art a general offense and every
man should beat thee. I think thou wast created for
men to breathe themselves upon thee.

Par. This is hard and undeserved measure, my lord.   270

Lafew. Go to, sir; you were beaten in Italy for picking a kernel out of a pomegranate; you are a vaga-
bond and no true traveler. You are more saucy with
lords and honorable personages than the commission
of your birth and virtue gives you heraldry. You are 275
not worth another word, else I'd call you knave. I
leave you.   *Exit.*

Par. Good, very good; it is so then. Good, very
good; let it be concealed awhile.

Enter Bertram.

Ber. Undone and forfeited to cares forever!   280

Par. What's the matter, sweetheart?

Ber. Although before the solemn priest I have
  sworn,
I will not bed her.

297. **curvet:** caper.

299. **jades:** nags.

303. **wherefore:** why.

307. **To:** compared to; **dark house:** prison or madhouse.

308. **capriccio:** whim.

310. **straight:** immediately.

312. **these balls bound:** this promises lively sport.

Par. What, what, sweetheart?   285
Ber. O my Parolles, they have married me!
I'll to the Tuscan wars and never bed her.
Par. France is a dog hole, and it no more merits
The tread of a man's foot: to the wars!
Ber. There's letters from my mother: 290
What the import is, I know not yet.
Par. Ay, that would be known. To the wars, my
    boy, to the wars!
He wears his honor in a box unseen,
That hugs his kicky-wicky here at home,   295
Spending his manly marrow in her arms
Which should sustain the bound and high curvet
Of Mars's fiery steed. To other regions
France is a stable, we that dwell in't jades:
Therefore, to the war!   300
Ber. It shall be so: I'll send her to my house,
Acquaint my mother with my hate to her
And wherefore I am fled; write to the King
That which I durst not speak. His present gift
Shall furnish me to those Italian fields   305
Where noble fellows strike. Wars is no strife
To the dark house and the detested wife.
Par. Will this capriccio hold in thee, art sure?
Ber. Go with me to my chamber and advise me.
I'll send her straight away: tomorrow   310
I'll to the wars, she to her single sorrow.
Par. Why, these balls bound; there's noise in it. 'Tis
    hard:
A young man married is a man that's marred.

316. hush 'tis so: we'd best say no more about that.

▰▰▰▰▰▰▰▰▰▰▰▰▰▰▰▰▰▰▰▰▰▰▰▰▰▰▰▰▰

II. iv. Helena receives the Countess' letter and Parolles then relays Bertram's order that she make her farewells to the King and leave that night. Bertram claims urgent business that calls him away but bids Helena convince the King that the departure is her own decision. Helena obediently promises to do as Bertram wishes.

45

Therefore away, and leave her bravely: go.   315
The King has done you wrong: but hush 'tis so.

Exeunt.

[Scene IV. Paris. The King's palace.]

Enter Helena and [Lavatch, the] Clown.

Hel. My mother greets me kindly: is she well?

Lav. She is not well; but yet she has her health.
She's very merry; but yet she is not well: but thanks
be given, she's very well and wants nothing i' the
world; but yet she is not well.   5

Hel. If she be very well, what does she ail, that
she's not very well?

Lav. Truly, she's very well indeed, but for two
things.

Hel. What two things?   10

Lav. One, that she's not in Heaven, whither God
send her quickly! the other, that she's in earth, from
whence God send her quickly!

Enter Parolles.

Par. Bless you, my fortunate lady!

Hel. I hope, sir, I have your good will to have mine 15
own good fortunes.

Par. You had my prayers to lead them on; and to
keep them on, have them still. O, my knave, how does
my old lady?

26. **title:** property (possession), with a pun on Parolles' name (French for *paroles*, words).

30. **Before me:** on my word (that is the word of a knave). Lavatch refers to the proverb "One false knave accuses another."

32. **found:** fathomed.

37. **well fed:** see II. ii. 3.

42. **puts it off to:** postpones it because of.

Lav. So that you had her wrinkles and I her money,   20
I would she did as you say.

Par. Why, I say nothing.

Lav. Marry, you are the wiser man; for many a
man's tongue shakes out his master's undoing. To say
nothing, to do nothing, to know nothing, and to have   25
nothing is to be a great part of your title; which is
within a very little of nothing.

Par. Away! th'art a knave.

Lav. You should have said, sir, "Before a knave
th'art a knave; that's, "Before me, th'art a knave":   30
this had been truth, sir.

Par. Go to, thou art a witty fool: I have found thee.

Lav. Did you find me in yourself, sir? or were you
taught to find me? The search, sir, was profitable; and
much fool may you find in you, even to the world's   35
pleasure and the increase of laughter.

Par. A good knave, i' faith, and well fed.
Madam, my lord will go away tonight;
A very serious business calls on him.
The great prerogative and rite of love,   40
Which, as your due, time claims, he does acknowledge;
But puts it off to a compelled restraint;
Whose want and whose delay is strewed with sweets,
Which they distill now in the curbed time,
To make the coming hour o'erflow with joy,   45
And pleasure drown the brim.

Hel.   What's his will else?

Par. That you will take your instant leave o' the
      King

50. **make this haste as your own good proceeding:** i.e., tell the King that this hasty departure is her own wish.

52. **make it probable need:** lend conviction to the excuse that necessity calls her away.

▬▬▬▬▬▬▬▬▬▬▬▬▬▬▬▬▬▬

II. v. Lafew tries to warn Bertram against Parolles, but Bertram is convinced of the braggart's valor and wisdom. Helena receives her husband's orders to return to Rossillion with a letter for his mother. Her timid request for a kiss is brushed aside, as Bertram orders haste in departing.

▬▬▬▬▬▬▬▬▬▬▬▬▬

3. **of very valiant approof:** proved very valiant by trial.

4. **deliverance:** report.

5. **warranted:** certified.

6-7. **dial:** watch; **lark for a bunting:** reversing the proverb "To take a bunting for a lark." Lafew means that if Bertram is right, he has done Parolles an injustice in his own estimate.

And make this haste as your own good proceeding,   50
Strengthened with what apology you think
May make it probable need.

   Hel.   What more commands he?

   Par. That, having this obtained, you presently
Attend his further pleasure.   55

   Hel. In everything I wait upon his will.

   Par. I shall report it so.

   Hel. I pray you. (*Exit Parolles.*) Come, sirrah.

                                  Exeunt.

[Scene V. The King's palace.]

Enter Lafew and Bertram.

   Lafew. But I hope your Lordship thinks not him a
soldier.

   Ber. Yes, my lord, and of very valiant approof.

   Lafew. You have it from his own deliverance.

   Ber. And by other warranted testimony.   5

   Lafew. Then my dial goes not true: I took this lark
for a bunting.

   Ber. I do assure you, my lord, he is very great in
knowledge and accordingly valiant.

   Lafew. I have then sinned against his experience   10
and transgressed against his valor; and my state that
way is dangerous, since I cannot yet find in my heart
to repent. Here he comes. I pray you, make us friends.
I will pursue the amity.

28-9. at the latter end of a dinner: i.e., to tell yarns.

38. him that leaped into the custard: i.e., a clown who performed this antic at a feast.

39-40. suffer question for your residence: discuss the reasons for your being in my displeasure.

Enter Parolles.

Par. [*To Bertram*] These things shall be done, sir.   15
Lafew. Pray you, sir, who's his tailor?
Par. Sir?
Lafew. O, I know him well, I, sir; he, sir, 's a good
workman, a very good tailor.

Ber. [*Aside to Parolles*] Is she gone to the King?   20
Par. She is.
Ber. Will she away tonight?
Par. As you'll have her.
Ber. I have writ my letters, casketed my treasure,
Given order for our horses; and tonight,   25
When I should take possession of the bride,
End ere I do begin.

Lafew. A good traveler is something at the latter
end of a dinner; but one that lies three thirds, and uses
a known truth to pass a thousand nothings with,   30
should be once heard and thrice beaten. God save
you, captain.

Ber. Is there any unkindness between my lord and
you, monsieur?

Par. I know not how I have deserved to run into my   35
lord's displeasure.

Lafew. You have made shift to run into't, boots and
spurs and all, like him that leaped into the custard;
and out of it you'll run again, rather than suffer question for your residence.   40

Ber. It may be you have mistaken him, my lord.

46. them: buffoons; **tame:** i.e., he has employed jesters in his household.

50. idle: foolish.

54. clog: hindrance.

61. holds not color with the time: does not befit the occasion of our recent marriage.

61-3. nor does /The ministration and required office /On my particular: nor does my course allow me to fulfill my duties as a husband.

68. respects: reasons.

Lafew. And shall do so ever, though I took him at 's prayers. Fare you well, my lord; and believe this of me, there can be no kernel in this light nut; the soul of this man is his clothes. Trust him not in matter of 45 heavy consequence. I have kept of them tame and know their natures. Farewell, monsieur: I have spoken better of you than you have or will to deserve at my hand; but we must do good against evil. [*Exit.*]

Par. An idle lord, I swear. 50

Ber. I think so.

Par. Why, do you not know him?

Ber. Yes, I do know him well, and common speech Gives him a worthy pass. Here comes my clog.

Enter Helena.

Hel. I have, sir, as I was commanded from you, 55
Spoke with the King and have procured his leave
For present parting; only he desires
Some private speech with you.

Ber.   I shall obey his will.
You must not marvel, Helen, at my course, 60
Which holds not color with the time, nor does
The ministration and required office
On my particular. Prepared I was not
For such a business; therefore am I found
So much unsettled. This drives me to entreat you 65
That presently you take your way for home,
And rather muse than ask why I entreat you;
For my respects are better than they seem,

78. **observance:** dedication.

78-80. **eke out that /Wherein toward me my homely stars have failed /To equal my great fortune:** compensate for my humble birth, which makes me unworthy of you.

85. **owe:** own.

And my appointments have in them a need
Greater than shows itself at the first view   70
To you that know them not. This to my mother:
                                        [*Giving a letter.*]
'Twill be two days ere I shall see you; so,
I leave you to your wisdom.
   Hel.   Sir, I can nothing say
But that I am your most obedient servant.   75
   Ber. Come, come, no more of that.
   Hel.   And ever shall
With true observance seek to eke out that
Wherein toward me my homely stars have failed
To equal my great fortune.   80
   Ber.   Let that go.
My haste is very great: farewell; hie home.
   Hel. Pray, sir, your pardon.
   Ber.   Well, what would you say?
   Hel. I am not worthy of the wealth I owe;   85
Nor dare I say 'tis mine, and yet it is;
But, like a timorous thief, most fain would steal
What law does vouch mine own.
   Ber.   What would you have?
   Hel. Something; and scarce so much: nothing, in-   90
     deed.
I would not tell you what I would, my lord.
Faith, yes,
Strangers and foes do sunder and not kiss.
   Ber. I pray you, stay not, but in haste to horse.   95
   Hel. I shall not break your bidding, good my lord.
   Ber. Where are my other men, monsieur? Farewell!
                                        Exit [*Helena*]

101. coraggio: Italian for "courage," one of the foreign words popular with men who had military experience abroad.

Go thou toward home; where I will never come
Whilst I can shake my sword or hear the drum.
Away, and for our flight.   100
   Par.   Bravely, *coraggio!*

                          Exeunt.

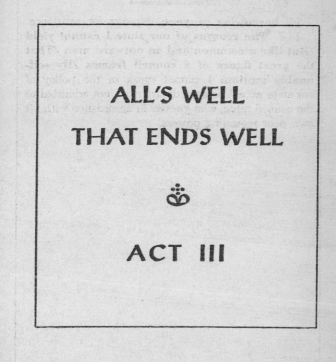

ALL'S WELL
THAT ENDS WELL

ACT III

III. i. The Duke of Florence welcomes the French lords and expresses disappointment that the King has refused him official aid.

━━━━━━━━━━━━━━━━━━━━━━━━━

12. **borrowing prayers:** requests for assistance.

14-7. **The reasons of our state I cannot yield /But like a common and an outward man /That the great figure of a council frames /By self-unable motion:** I cannot speak of the policy of our state except as an ordinary man, not admitted to the council table, who guesses in accordance with his own poor reasoning powers.

ACT III

Scene I. [Florence. The Duke's palace.]

*Flourish. Enter the Duke of Florence, the two
Frenchmen, with a troop of soldiers.*

Duke. So that from point to point now have you
    heard
The fundamental reasons of this war,
Whose great decision hath much blood let forth,
And more thirsts after.   5

1. Lo.   Holy seems the quarrel
Upon your Grace's part; black and fearful
On the opposer.

Duke. Therefore we marvel much our cousin
    France   10
Would in so just a business shut his bosom
Against our borrowing prayers.

2. Lo.   Good my lord,
The reasons of our state I cannot yield
But like a common and an outward man   15
That the great figure of a council frames
By self-unable motion: therefore dare not

52

22. **of our nature:** like himself and his comrade, who desire action.

28. **When better fall, for your avails they fell:** i.e., when better places become available, they will be yours.

III. ii. Bertram's letter to the Countess informs her that he has run away from his unwelcome wife and is determined not to live with her. Helena, too, has had a letter in which Bertram declares that she may call him "husband" only after she has secured his ring and given birth to his child, something that he does not intend to happen. The Countess is shocked at her son's behavior and prepares to send him a message expressing her disapproval. Helena, conscience-stricken at the thought that her presence at Rossillion has sent her husband into the dangers of battle, resolves to vanish so that he need not stay away on her account.

Say what I think of it, since I have found
Myself in my incertain grounds to fail
As often as I guessed.   20

Duke.   Be it his pleasure.

1. Lo. But I am sure the younger of our nature,
That surfeit on their ease, will day by day
Come here for physic.

Duke.   Welcome shall they be;   25
And all the honors that can fly from us
Shall on them settle. You know your places well;
When better fall, for your avails they fell.
Tomorrow to the field.

                                   Flourish. [*Exeunt.*]

[Scene II. Rossillion. The Count's palace.]

Enter Countess and [*Lavatch, the*] *Clown.*

Coun. It hath happened all as I would have had
it, save that he comes not along with her.

Lav. By my troth, I take my young lord to be a
very melancholy man.

Coun. By what observance, I pray you?   5

Lav. Why, he will look upon his boot and sing;
mend the ruff and sing; ask questions and sing; pick
his teeth and sing. I know a man that had this trick
of melancholy sold a goodly manor for a song.

Coun. Let me see what he writes and when he   10
means to come.

13. **lings:** salt cod; i.e., lust.

32. **the contempt of empire:** an emperor's contempt.

33. **heavy:** sorrowful.

Lav. I have no mind to Isbel since I was at court.
Our old lings and our Isbels o' the country are nothing like your old lings and your Isbels o' the court.
The brains of my Cupid's knocked out, and I begin to   15
love, as an old man loves money, with no stomach.

Coun. What have we here?

Lav. E'en that you have there.   *Exit.*

Coun. [*Reads*] "I have sent you a daughter-in-
law: she hath recovered the King and undone me.   20
I have wedded her, not bedded her, and sworn to
make the 'not' eternal. You shall hear I am run away:
know it before the report come. If there be breadth
enough in the world, I will hold a long distance. My
duty to you.   25

                    Your unfortunate son,
                        BERTRAM."

This is not well, rash and unbridled boy,
To fly the favors of so good a King;
To pluck his indignation on thy head   30
By the misprizing of a maid too virtuous
For the contempt of empire.

            Enter [Lavatch, the] Clown.

Lav. O madam, yonder is heavy nows within between two soldiers and my young lady!

Coun. What is the matter?   35

Lav. Nay, there is some comfort in the news, some
comfort: your son will not be killed so soon as I
thought he would.

50. **on the start:** appearing unexpectedly.

51. **woman me unto't:** provoke an emotional display such as women are reputed to show.

55. **some dispatch in hand:** dispatch of some business in hand.

57. **passport:** i.e., license to beg, such as were given to the deserving poor who were unable to support themselves.

Coun. Why should he be killed?

Lav. So say I, madam, if he run away, as I hear he   40
does. The danger is in standing to't; that's the loss
of men, though it be the getting of children. Here
they come will tell you more. For my part, I only
hear your son was run away.   [*Exit.*]

Enter Helena and two Gentlemen.

1. Gent. Save you, good madam.   45

Hel. Madam, my lord is gone, forever gone.

2. Gent. Do not say so.

Coun. Think upon patience. Pray you, gentlemen,
I have felt so many quirks of joy and grief,
That the first face of neither, on the start,   50
Can woman me unto't. Where is my son, I pray you?

2. Gent. Madam, he's gone to serve the Duke of
        Florence:
We met him thitherward; for thence we came,
And, after some dispatch in hand at court,   55
Thither we bend again.

Hel. Look on his letter, madam; here's my passport.
[*Reads*] "When thou canst get the ring upon my
finger, which never shall come off, and show me a
child begotten of thy body that I am father to,   60
then call me husband: but in such a 'then' I write
a 'never.'"
This is a dreadful sentence.

Coun. Brought you this letter, gentlemen?

1. Gent.   Ay, madam;   65

68. **engrossest all the griefs are thine:** try to monopolize grief.

69. **moiety:** share.

71. **all my:** my only.

76. **good convenience claims:** is appropriate to his deserts.

85. **haply:** perhaps.

And for the contents' sake are sorry for our pains.

   Coun. I prithee, lady, have a better cheer:
If thou engrossest all the griefs are thine,
Thou robbest me of a moiety. He was my son;
But I do wash his name out of my blood   70
And thou art all my child. Towards Florence is he?

   2. Gent. Ay, madam.

   Coun.   And to be a soldier?

   2. Gent. Such is his noble purpose; and, believe't,
The Duke will lay upon him all the honor   75
That good convenience claims.

   Coun.   Return you thither?

   1. Gent. Ay, madam, with the swiftest wing of
    speed.

   Hel. [*Reads*] "Till I have no wife, I have nothing 80
    in France."
'Tis bitter.

   Coun. Find you that there?

   Hel.   Ay, madam.

   1. Gent. 'Tis but the boldness of his hand, haply, 85
which his heart was not consenting to.

   Coun. Nothing in France, until he have no wife!
There's nothing here that is too good for him
But only she; and she deserves a lord
That twenty such rude boys might tend upon   90
And call her hourly mistress. Who was with him?

   1. Gent. A servant only, and a gentleman
Which I have sometime known.

   Coun.   Parolles, was it not?

   1. Gent. Ay, my good lady, he.   95

101-2. **a deal of that too much, /Which holds him much to have:** a deal too much of that **inducement,** which he uses for his advantage.

110. **Not so, but as we change our courtesies:** only if I may requite you with equal service.

118. **event:** outcome; chance.

124. **still peering air:** air that seems not to move (and is in fact invulnerable).

Coun. A very tainted fellow and full of wicked-
    ness.
My son corrupts a well-derived nature
With his inducement.

1. Gent.   Indeed, good lady,   100
The fellow has a deal of that too much,
Which holds him much to have.

Coun. Y' are welcome, gentlemen.
I will entreat you, when you see my son,
To tell him that his sword can never win   105
The honor that he loses: more I'll entreat you
Written to bear along.

2. Gent. We serve you, madam,
In that and all your worthiest affairs.

Coun. Not so, but as we change our courtesies.   110
Will you draw near?

                Exeunt [Countess and Gentlemen].
Hel. "Till I have no wife, I have nothing in
    France."
Nothing in France, until he has no wife!
Thou shalt have none, Rossillion, none in France;   115
Then hast thou all again. Poor lord! is't I
That chase thee from thy country and expose
Those tender limbs of thine to the event
Of the none-sparing war? and is it I
That drive thee from the sportive court, where thou   120
Wast shot at with fair eyes, to be the mark
Of smoky muskets? O you leaden messengers,
That ride upon the violent speed of fire,
Fly with false aim; move the still peering air,

125. **sings with piercing:** the implied metaphor is that the bullet makes the air sing.

126. **set him there:** made him the target.

128. **caitiff:** guilty wretch.

131. **ravin:** ravenous.

135. **but of danger wins a scar:** i.e., wins of danger but a scar.

140. **officed all:** performed all the domestic services.

III. [iii.] Bertram has so distinguished himself in action that the Duke of Florence appoints him general of his horse.

Rumor personified. From Henry Peacham, *Minerva Britanna* (1618).

That sings with piercing; do not touch my lord.   125
Whoever shoots at him, I set him there;
Whoever charges on his forward breast,
I am the caitiff that do hold him to't;
And, though I kill him not, I am the cause
His death was so effected. Better 'twere   130
I met the ravin lion when he roared
With sharp constraint of hunger; better 'twere
That all the miseries which nature owes
Were mine at once. No, come thou home, Rossillion,
Whence honor but of danger wins a scar,   135
As oft it loses all. I will be gone;
My being here it is that holds thee hence.
Shall I stay here to do't? No, no, although
The air of paradise did fan the house,
And angels officed all. I will be gone,   140
That pitiful Rumor may report my flight,
To consolate thine ear. Come, night; end, day!
For with the dark, poor thief, I'll steal away.

Exit.

[Scene III. Florence. Before the Duke's palace.]

*Flourish. Enter the Duke of Florence, Bertram,
  Parolles, Soldiers, Drum, and Trumpets.*

Duke. The general of our horse thou art; and we,
Great in our hope, lay our best love and credence
Upon thy promising fortune.
   Ber.   Sir, it is

9. **helm:** helmet.

III. iv. Helena, having informed the Countess by letter that she has undertaken a pilgrimage to St. James of Compostela in penance for her ambitious love for Bertram, urges her to write Bertram that he may come home. The Countess regrets that she did not anticipate Helena's flight and orders her steward to write a letter to Bertram reporting his wife's departure and stressing her virtues and his unworthiness.

4. **St. Jaques:** St. James the Greater; his shrine at Compostela, Spain, was visited by many pilgrims.

59

A charge too heavy for my strength, but yet   5
We'll strive to bear it for your worthy sake
To the extreme edge of hazard.
   Duke.   Then go thou forth;
And Fortune play upon thy prosperous helm,
As thy auspicious mistress!   10
   Ber.   This very day,
Great Mars, I put myself into thy file:
Make me but like my thoughts and I shall prove
A lover of thy drum, hater of love.
                           Exeunt omnes.

[Scene IV. Rossillion. The Count's palace.]

Enter Countess and [Rinaldo, the] Steward.

   Coun. Alas! and would you take the letter of her?
Might you not know she would do as she has done,
By sending me a letter? Read it again.
   Rin. [*Reads*]
"I am St. Jaques' pilgrim, thither gone:
   Ambitious love hath so in me offended,   5
That barefoot plod I the cold ground upon,
   With sainted vow my faults to have amended.
Write, write, that from the bloody course of war
   My dearest master, your dear son, may hie.
Bless him at home in peace, whilst I from far   10
   His name with zealous fervor sanctify.
His taken labors bid him me forgive.

13. **his despiteful Juno:** Juno was the jealous wife of Jupiter. Her hostility to Hercules, Jupiter's son by Alcmene, resulted in the imposition of the twelve labors Hercules performed for Eurystheus.

17. **Whom:** i.e., death.

20. **lack advice so much:** so fail in good judgment.

25. **at overnight:** last night.

The labors of Hercules. From Ovid, *Metamorphoses* (1522).

   I, his despiteful Juno, sent him forth
From courtly friends with camping foes to live,
   Where death and danger dogs the heels of worth.   15
He is too good and fair for death and me,
Whom I myself embrace to set him free."
   Coun. Ah, what sharp stings are in her mildest
      words!
Rinaldo, you did never lack advice so much   20
As letting her pass so. Had I spoke with her,
I could have well diverted her intents,
Which thus she hath prevented.
   Rin.   Pardon me, madam.
If I had given you this at overnight,   25
She might have been o'erta'en; and yet she writes
Pursuit would be but vain.
   Coun.   What angel shall
Bless this unworthy husband? He cannot thrive,
Unless her prayers whom Heaven delights to hear   30
And loves to grant reprieve him from the wrath
Of greatest justice. Write, write, Rinaldo,
To this unworthy husband of his wife;
Let every word weigh heavy of her worth
That he does weigh too light: my greatest grief,   35
Though little he do feel it, set down sharply.
Dispatch the most convenient messenger.
When haply he shall hear that she is gone,
He will return; and hope I may that she,
Hearing so much, will speed her foot again,   40
Led hither by pure love: which of them both
Is dearest to me, I have no skill in sense

III. v. Helena goes to Florence, where she meets Diana Capilet and her mother and learns that Bertram has been courting Diana. Diana's mother keeps a hostel for pilgrims, where Helena agrees to lodge, promising to impart something to Diana that will be worth her while.

▬▬▬▬▬▬▬▬▬▬▬▬▬▬▬▬▬▬▬▬

Ent.: this stage direction in the Folio has "Violenta" as the name of the Widow's daughter; **tucket:** trumpet call.

17. **officer:** agent; **suggestions:** enticements.

To make distinction. Provide this messenger.
My heart is heavy and mine age is weak;
Grief would have tears, and sorrow bids me speak.   45
                                        Exeunt.

[Scene V. Florence. Without the walls.]

*A tucket afar off. Enter an old Widow of Florence,
her daughter [Diana], and Mariana, with other
                    Citizens.*

Wid. Nay, come; for if they do approach the city,
we shall lose all the sight.

Dia. They say the French count has done most
honorable service.

Wid. It is reported that he has taken their great'st   5
commander and that with his own hand he slew the
Duke's brother. [*Tucket.*] We have lost our labor;
they are gone a contrary way. Hark! you may know
by their trumpets.

Mar. Come, let's return again and suffice ourselves   10
with the report of it. Well, Diana, take heed of this
French earl: the honor of a maid is her name; and no
legacy is so rich as honesty.

Wid. I have told my neighbor how you have been
solicited by a gentleman his companion.   15

Mar. I know that knave, hang him! one Parolles:
a filthy officer he is in those suggestions for the young
earl. Beware of them, Diana: their promises, entice-

19. **engines:** snares.

20. **go under:** pretend to be.

23. **succession:** those who come later.

24. **limed:** caught, like birds in birdlime.

26. **grace:** virtue.

35. **palmers:** pilgrims; the term was originally applied to those who had traveled to the Holy Land and bore palm leaves in token of the pilgrimage. The pilgrim to Compostela wore a scallop shell in the hat.

36. **port:** gate.

44. **ample:** amply; well.

A pilgrim to the shrine of St. James of Compostela. From Henry Peacham, *Minerva Britanna* (1618).

ments, oaths, tokens, and all these engines of lust are
not the things they go under. Many a maid hath   20
been seduced by them; and the misery is, example,
that so terrible shows in the wrack of maidenhood,
cannot for all that dissuade succession but that they
are limed with the twigs that threatens them. I hope
I need not to advise you further; but I hope your   25
own grace will keep you where you are, though
there were no further danger known but the modesty which is so lost.

Dia. You shall not need to fear me.

Enter Helena, [disguised as a Pilgrim].

Wid. I hope so. Look, here comes a pilgrim. I   30
know she will lie at my house; thither they send one
another. I'll question her. God save you, pilgrim!
whither are you bound?

Hel. To St. Jaques le Grand.
Where do the palmers lodge, I do beseech you?   35

Wid. At the St. Francis here beside the port.

Hel. Is this the way?

Wid. Ay, marry, is't. [*A march afar.*] Hark you!
    they come this way.
If you will tarry, holy pilgrim,   40
But till the troops come by,
I will conduct you where you shall be lodged;
The rather, for I think I know your hostess
As ample as myself.

57. **He's bravely taken:** he has a splendid reputation.
58. **for:** because.
60. **mere the truth:** the absolute truth.
68. **all her deserving:** her sole virtue.
69. **reserved honesty:** preserved virginity.
70. **examined:** questioned; doubted.

Hel.   Is it yourself?   45
Wid. If you shall please so, pilgrim.
Hel. I thank you, and will stay upon your leisure.
Wid. You came, I think, from France?
Hel.   I did so.
Wid. Here you shall see a countryman of yours   50
That has done worthy service.
Hel.   His name, I pray you?
Dia. The Count Rossillion: know you such a one?
Hel. But by the ear, that hears most nobly of him;
His face I know not.   55
Dia.   Whatsome'er he is,
He's bravely taken here. He stole from France,
As 'tis reported, for the King had married him
Against his liking. Think you it is so?
Hel. Ay, surely, mere the truth; I know his lady.   60
Dia. There is a gentleman that serves the Count
Reports but coarsely of her.
Hel.   What's his name?
Dia. Monsieur Parolles.
Hel.   O, I believe with him,   65
In argument of praise, or to the worth
Of the great Count himself, she is too mean
To have her name repeated; all her deserving
Is a reserved honesty, and that
I have not heard examined.   70
Dia.   Alas, poor lady!
'Tis a hard bondage to become the wife
Of a detesting lord.
Wid. I warrant, good creature, wheresoe'er she is,

77. **shrewd turn:** evil trick; wrong.
82. **brokes:** bargains; haggles.
93. **honester:** more honorable.

Her heart weighs sadly. This young maid might do   75
    her
A shrewd turn, if she pleased.
    Hel.   How do you mean?
May be the amorous Count solicits her
In the unlawful purpose.   80
    Wid.   He does indeed;
And brokes with all that can in such a suit
Corrupt the tender honor of a maid;
But she is armed for him and keeps her guard
In honestest defense.   85
    Mar.   The gods forbid else!
    Wid. So, now they come:

*Drum and Colors. Enter Bertram, Parolles, and the
            whole army.*

That is Antonio, the Duke's eldest son;
That, Escalus.
    Hel.   Which is the Frenchman?   90
    Dia.   He;
That with the plume. 'Tis a most gallant fellow.
I would he loved his wife. If he were honester
He were much goodlier. Is't not a handsome gentle-
    man?   95
    Hel. I like him well.
    Dia. 'Tis pity he is not honest. Yond's that same
    knave
That leads him to these places. Were I his lady,
I would poison that vile rascal.   100

106. **shrewdly:** grievously; extremely.

109. **ring-carrier:** one who acts as a go-between in a love affair; a bawd.

112. **host:** lodge; **enjoined penitents:** travelers whose pilgrimages have been prescribed as penance for their sins.

116. **Please it:** if it please.

117-18. **the charge and thanking /Shall be for me:** I will assume both the cost and the burden of gratitude for your courtesy.

118. **requite:** reward.

119. **of:** on.

▬▬▬▬▬▬▬▬▬▬▬▬▬▬▬▬▬▬

III. vi. Two French lords seek to reveal Parolles' cowardice and villainy to Bertram. They contrive a plot whereby Parolles will be encouraged to try to recapture a drum lost to the enemy. They plan to disguise themselves and take him prisoner, at which time his lack of valor will be displayed. Bertram agrees to the plan and discloses that he is still besieging Diana.

▬▬▬▬▬▬▬▬▬▬▬▬

1. **to't:** to trial.

Hel.   Which is he?

Dia. That jackanapes with scarves. Why is he melancholy?

Hel. Perchance he's hurt i' the battle.

Par. Lose our drum! well.   105

Mar. He's shrewdly vexed at something. Look, he has spied us.

Wid. Marry, hang you!

Mar. And your courtesy, for a ring-carrier!

                    Exeunt [*Bertram, Parolles, and army*].

Wid. The troop is past. Come, pilgrim, I will bring 110
  you
Where you shall host. Of enjoined penitents
There's four or five, to Great St. Jaques bound,
Already at my house.

Hel.   I humbly thank you.   115
Please it this matron and this gentle maid
To eat with us tonight, the charge and thanking
Shall be for me; and, to requite you further,
I will bestow some precepts of this virgin
Worthy the note.   120

Both.   We'll take your offer kindly.

                                        Exeunt.

_____

[Scene VI. Camp before Florence.]

Enter Bertram and the two French Lords.

2. *Lo.* Nay, good my lord, put him to't; let him
have his way.

3. **hilding:** coward.

5. **bubble:** showy nothing; sham.

9. **as my kinsman:** i.e., with the partiality of a relative, which the gentleman is not.

12. **entertainment:** support; maintenance.

18. **fetch off:** rescue.

22. **surprise:** capture.

23-4. **hoodwink:** blindfold.

25. **leaguer:** camp (Dutch *leger*).

1. Lo. If your Lordship find him not a hilding, hold me no more in your respect.

2. Lo. On my life, my lord, a bubble.   5

Ber. Do you think I am so far deceived in him?

2. Lo. Believe it, my lord, in mine own direct knowledge, without any malice, but to speak of him as my kinsman, he's a most notable coward, an infinite and endless liar, an hourly promise-breaker,   10 the owner of no one good quality worthy your Lordship's entertainment.

1. Lo. It were fit you knew him, lest, reposing too far in his virtue, which he hath not, he might at some great and trusty business in a main danger fail you.   15

Ber. I would I knew in what particular action to try him.

1. Lo. None better than to let him fetch off his drum, which you hear him so confidently undertake to do.   20

2. Lo. I, with a troop of Florentines, will suddenly surprise him; such I will have whom I am sure he knows not from the enemy. We will bind and hoodwink him so that he shall suppose no other but that he is carried into the leaguer of the adversaries, when   25 we bring him to our own tents. Be but your Lordship present at his examination; if he do not, for the promise of his life and in the highest compulsion of base fear, offer to betray you and deliver all the intelligence in his power against you, and that with   30 the divine forfeit of his soul upon oath, never trust my judgment in anything.

37-8. John Drum's entertainment: i.e., a good beating. This is apparently a proverbial phrase, possibly from an old tale.

38. inclining: i.e., attachment to Parolles.

41-2. in any hand: anyhow; regardless.

45. A pox on't: plague take it.

48. wings: flanking detachments.

Martial drummers. From Geoffrey Whitney, *A Choice of Emblems* (1586).

1. Lo. O, for the love of laughter, let him fetch his
drum; he says he has a stratagem for't. When your
Lordship sees the bottom of his success in't, and to   35
what metal this counterfeit lump of ore will be
melted, if you give him not John Drum's entertainment, your inclining cannot be removed. Here he
comes.

Enter Parolles.

2. Lo. O, for the love of laughter, hinder not the   40
honor of his design: let him fetch off his drum in any
hand.

Ber. How now, monsieur! this drum sticks sorely
in your disposition.

1. Lo. A pox on't, let it go; 'tis but a drum.   45

Par. But a drum! Is't but a drum? A drum so lost!
There was excellent command—to charge in with our
horse upon our own wings, and to rend our own
soldiers!

1. Lo. That was not to be blamed in the command   50
of the service: it was a disaster of war that Caesar
himself could not have prevented, if he had been
there to command.

Ber. Well, we cannot greatly condemn our success:
some dishonor we had in the loss of that drum, but it   55
is not to be recovered.

Par. It might have been recovered.

Ber. It might; but it is not now.

Par. It is to be recovered. But that the merit of

61-2. **hic jacet:** (write) "here lies" (on my tomb-stone).

63. **a stomach:** the courage.

64. **mystery:** craft.

66. **magnanimous:** valiant to a high degree; nobly brave.

67. **grace:** honor.

74. **dilemmas:** difficulties.

75. **put myself into my mortal preparation:** prepare myself for death.

81. **possibility:** potentiality.

82. **subscribe:** vouch.

service is seldom attributed to the true and exact per- 60
former, I would have that drum or another, or *hic
jacet*.

Ber. Why, if you have a stomach, to't, monsieur.
If you think your mystery in stratagem can bring
this instrument of honor again into his native 65
quarter, be magnanimous in the enterprise and go on.
I will grace the attempt for a worthy exploit. If you
speed well in it, the Duke shall both speak of it and
extend to you what further becomes his greatness,
even to the utmost syllable of your worthiness. 70

Par. By the hand of a soldier, I will undertake it.

Ber. But you must not now slumber in it.

Par. I'll about it this evening; and I will presently
pen down my dilemmas, encourage myself in my
certainty, put myself into my mortal preparation; 75
and by midnight look to hear further from me.

Ber. May I be bold to acquaint His Grace you are
gone about it?

Par. I know not what the success will be, my lord;
but the attempt I vow. 80

Ber. I know th'art valiant and to the possibility of
thy soldiership will subscribe for thee. Farewell.

Par. I love not many words.   *Exit.*

2. Lo. No more than a fish loves water. Is not this
a strange fellow, my lord, that so confidently seems 85
to undertake this business, which he knows is not to
be done, damns himself to do, and dares better be
damned than to do't?

1. Lo. You do not know him, my lord, as we do.

99. **embossed him:** literally, "driven him to extremity" (like an animal pursued by hunters); that is, captured him.

103. **case:** skin; expose; **smoked:** detected; recognized for what he is.

105. **sprat:** contemptible object.

107. **look:** seek; **twigs:** on which to spread birdlime; see III. v. 24.

116. **coxcomb:** fool; **have i' the wind:** are near to catching (like an animal who cannot scent the hunter to windward of him).

certain it is that he will steal himself into a man's 90
favor and for a week escape a great deal of discoveries; but when you find him out, you have him
ever after.

Ber. Why, do you think he will make no deed at
all of this that so seriously he does address himself 95
unto?

2. Lo. None in the world; but return with an invention and clap upon you two or three probable lies.
But we have almost embossed him; you shall see his
fall tonight; for indeed he is not for your Lordship's 100
respect.

1. Lo. We'll make you some sport with the fox ere
we case him. He was first smoked by the old Lord
Lafew. When his disguise and he is parted, tell me
what a sprat you shall find him; which you shall see 105
this very night.

2. Lo. I must go look my twigs; he shall be caught.

Ber. Your brother, he shall go along with me.

2. Lo. As't please your Lordship. I'll leave you.
[*Exit.*]

Ber. Now will I lead you to the house and show 110
you

The lass I spoke of.

1. Lo.   But you say she's honest.

Ber. That's all the fault. I spoke with her but once
And found her wondrous cold; but I sent to her, 115
By this same coxcomb that we have i' the wind,
Tokens and letters which she did re-send;
And this is all I have done. She's a fair creature.

III. vii. Helena reveals herself to the Widow Capilet as the wife of Bertram and suggests that Diana pretend to yield, demand his ring as a pledge, and make an assignation, which Helena will keep. For this deception she promises to provide Diana with a dowry of 3,000 crowns.

1. **misdoubt:** suspect.
3. **the grounds I work upon:** i.e., the concealment of her identity from Bertram.
10. **counsel:** secrecy.
11. **from word to word:** entirely; to the letter.

Will you go see her?

1. *Lo.*   With all my heart, my lord.   120

Exeunt.

[Scene VII. Florence. The Widow's house.]

Enter Helena and Widow.

Hel. If you misdoubt me that I am not she,
I know not how I shall assure you further,
But I shall lose the grounds I work upon.

Wid. Though my estate be fall'n, I was well born,
Nothing acquainted with these businesses,   5
And would not put my reputation now
In any staining act.

Hel.   Nor would I wish you.
First give me trust the Count he is my husband,
And what to your sworn counsel I have spoken   10
Is so from word to word; and then you cannot,
By the good aid that I of you shall borrow,
Err in bestowing it.

Wid.   I should believe you;
For you have showed me that which well approves   15
Y'are great in fortune.

Hel.   Take this purse of gold,
And let me buy your friendly help thus far,
Which I will overpay and pay again
When I have found it. The Count he woos your   20
    daughter,

23. **in fine:** finally.

25. **important blood:** importunate passion.

26. **County:** Count.

29-30. **holds /In most rich choice:** considers very precious.

30. **idle fire:** foolish passion.

31. **will:** satisfaction of his lust.

40. **To marry her:** as a dowry.

47. **To her unworthiness:** designed to appeal to the least worthy part of her nature; **steads:** avails.

Lays down his wanton siege before her beauty,
Resolves to carry her: let her in fine consent,
As we'll direct her how 'tis best to bear it.
Now his important blood will nought deny   25
That she'll demand: a ring the County wears
That downward hath succeeded in his house
From son to son, some four or five descents
Since the first father wore it. This ring he holds
In most rich choice; yet in his idle fire,   30
To buy his will, it would not seem too dear,
Howe'er repented after.

   Wid.   Now I see
The bottom of your purpose.

   Hel. You see it lawful, then: it is no more   35
But that your daughter, ere she seems as won,
Desires this ring; appoints him an encounter;
In fine, delivers me to fill the time,
Herself most chastely absent. After,
To marry her, I'll add three thousand crowns   40
To what is past already.

   Wid.   I have yielded:
Instruct my daughter how she shall persever,
That time and place with this deceit so lawful
May prove coherent. Every night he comes   45
With musics of all sorts and songs composed
To her unworthiness: it nothing steads us
To chide him from our eaves, for he persists
As if his life lay on't.

   Hel.   Why then tonight   50
Let us assay our plot; which, if it speed,

52-3. wicked meaning in a lawful deed, /And lawful meaning in a lawful act: Bertram's meaning is wicked in wishing to seduce a girl to whom he is not married; Helena's is the lawful meaning in wishing to sleep with her own husband, a lawful act.

54. fact: crime. Bertram's deed will be sinful in intent, since he will not know the woman to be his wife.

Is wicked meaning in a lawful deed,
And lawful meaning in a lawful act,
Where both not sin, and yet a sinful fact.
But let's about it.   55

Exeunt.

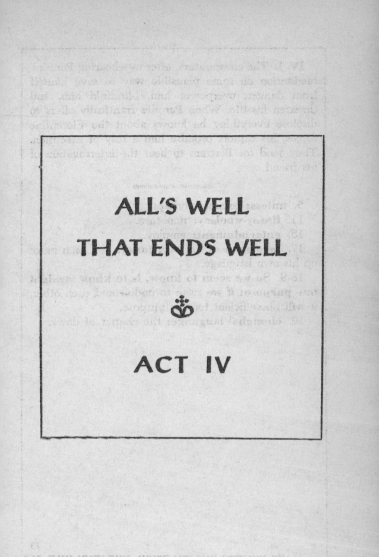

ALL'S WELL
THAT ENDS WELL

ACT IV

IV. i. The conspirators, after overhearing Parolles'
meditation on some plausible way to save himself
from danger, overpower him, blindfold him, and
threaten his life. When Parolles frantically offers to
disclose everything he knows about the Florentine
forces, his captors promise him a stay of execution.
They send for Bertram to hear the interrogation of
his friend.

5. **unless:** except, perhaps.

11. **linsey-woolsey:** nonsense.

15. **entertainment:** employ.

17. **be a man of his own fancy:** i.e., each make
up his own language.

18-9. **So we seem to know, is to know straight
our purpose:** if we seem to understand each other,
it will be sufficient for our purpose.

19. **choughs' language:** the chatter of daws.

ACT IV

[Scene I. Without the Florentine camp.]

Enter one of the Frenchmen [Second French Lord,]
with five or six other Soldiers in ambush.

2. *Lo.* He can come no other way but by this
hedge corner. When you sally upon him, speak what
terrible language you will. Though you understand it
not yourselves, no matter; for we must not seem to
understand him, unless some one among us whom we   5
must produce for an interpreter.

1. *Sold.* Good captain, let me be the interpreter.

2. *Lo.* Art not acquainted with him? knows he not
thy voice?

1. *Sold.* No, sir, I warrant you.   10

2. *Lo.* But what linsey-woolsey hast thou to speak
to us again?

1. *Sold.* E'en such as you speak to me.

2. *Lo.* He must think us some band of strangers i'
the adversary's entertainment. Now he hath a smack   15
of all neighboring languages; therefore we must every
one be a man of his own fancy, not to know what we
speak one to another. So we seem to know, is to know
straight our purpose: choughs' language, gabble

21. **politic:** crafty; **couch, ho:** let's hide ourselves.

22. **beguile:** while away.

26. **plausive:** plausible.

27. **smoke:** see through, as at III. vi. 103.

30-1. **not daring the reports of my tongue:** not matching my tongue in daring.

40. **what's the instance:** how shall I proceed.

41. **butter-woman:** proverbially reputed to be a scold.

42. **Bajazet:** the Turkish sultan in Christopher Marlowe's *Tamburlaine*.

enough and good enough. As for you, interpreter, you 20
must seem very politic. But couch, ho! here he comes,
to beguile two hours in a sleep and then to return
and swear the lies he forges.

Enter Parolles.

Par. Ten o'clock: within these three hours 'twill be
time enough to go home. What shall I say I have 25
done? It must be a very plausive invention that carries it. They begin to smoke me, and disgraces have of
late knocked too often at my door. I find my tongue is
too foolhardy; but my heart hath the fear of Mars before it and of his creatures, not daring the reports of 30
my tongue.

2. Lo. This is the first truth that e'er thine own
tongue was guilty of.

Par. What the Devil should move me to undertake
the recovery of this drum, being not ignorant of the 35
impossibility and knowing I had no such purpose? I
must give myself some hurts and say I got them in
exploit: yet slight ones will not carry it. They will say,
"Came you off with so little?" And great ones I dare
not give. Wherefore, what's the instance? Tongue, I 40
must put you into a butter-woman's mouth and buy
myself another of Bajazet's mute, if you prattle me
into these perils.

2. Lo. Is it possible he should know what he is and
be that he is? 45

Par. I would the cutting of my garments would
serve the turn, or the breaking of my Spanish sword.

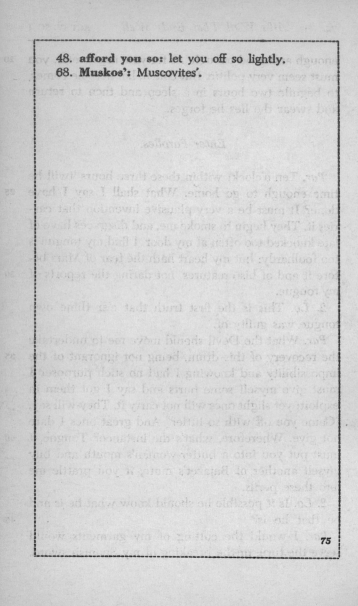

48. **afford you so**: let you off so lightly.
68. **Muskos'**: Muscovites'.

2. *Lo*. We cannot afford you so.

Par. Or the baring of my beard; and to say it was
in stratagem. 50

1. *Lo*. 'Twould not do.

Par. Or to drown my clothes and say I was stripped.

2. *Lo*. Hardly serve.

Par. Though I swore I leaped from the window of
the citadel— 55

2. *Lo*. How deep?

Par. Thirty fathom.

2. *Lo*. Three great oaths would scarce make that be
believed.

Par. I would I had any drum of the enemy's; I 60
would swear I recovered it.

2. *Lo*. You shall hear one anon.

Par. A drum now of the enemy's!   *Alarum within*.

2. *Lo*. Throca movousus, cargo, cargo, cargo.

All. Cargo, cargo, cargo, villianda par corbo, cargo. 65

Par. O, ransom, ransom! do not hide mine eyes.
            [*They seize and blindfold him*.]

1. *Sold*. Boskos thromuldo boskos.

Par. I know you are the Muskos' regiment;
And I shall lose my life for want of language.
If there be here German, or Dane, Low Dutch, 70
Italian, or French, let him speak to me.
I'll discover that which shall undo the Florentine.

1. *Sold*. Boskos vauvado:
I understand thee and can speak thy tongue.
Kerelybonto, sir 75
Betake thee to thy faith, for seventeen poniards
Are at thy bosom.

83. **hoodwinked:** blindfolded.
93. **space:** time.
95. **woodcock:** dupe; fool.
99. **'A:** he.

Par.   O!

1. Sold.   O, pray, pray, pray!

Manka revania dulche.   80

2. Lo. Oscorbidulchos volivorco.

1. Sold. The general is content to spare thee yet;
And, hoodwinked as thou art, will lead thee on
To gather from thee: haply thou mayst inform
Something to save thy life.   85

Par.   O, let me live!
And all the secrets of our camp I'll show,
Their force, their purposes; nay, I'll speak that
Which you will wonder at.

1. Sold.   But wilt thou faithfully? 90

Par. If I do not, damn me.

1. Sold. Acordo linta.

Come on; thou art granted space.

Exit, [with Parolles guarded]. A short alarum within.

2. Lo. Go, tell the Count Rossillion and my brother
We have caught the woodcock and will keep him 95
     muffled
Till we do hear from them.

2. Sold.   Captain, I will.

2. Lo. 'A will betray us all unto ourselves:
Inform on that.   100

2. Sold. So I will, sir.

2. Lo. Till then I'll keep him dark and safely
     locked.

                              Exeunt.

IV. ii. Bertram has a meeting with Diana, who pretends to yield to his ardor and secures Bertram's ring; in return she promises to admit him to her bed that night.

---

3. **Titled goddess:** called by a goddess' name.

4. **addition:** additional titles.

5. **In your fine frame hath love no quality:** can you see no excellence in love.

7. **monument:** statue.

11. **got:** conceived.

12. **honest:** i.e., not technically unchaste, since she was married.

20. **constraint:** compulsion.

24. **barely:** merely; i.e., leave us unprotected and exposed to shame and regret.

[Scene II. Florence. The Widow's house.]

Enter Bertram and the maid called Diana.

Ber. They told me that your name was Fontibell.
Dia. No, my good lord, Diana.
Ber.   Titled goddess;
And worth it, with additiunl But, fair soul,
In your fine frame hath love no quality?   5
If the quick fire of youth light not your mind,
You are no maiden but a monument.
When you are dead, you should be such a one
As you are now, for you are cold and stern;
And now you should be as your mother was   10
When your sweet self was got.
Dia. She then was honest.
Ber.   So should you be.
Dia.   No:
My mother did but duty; such, my lord,   15
As you owe to your wife.
Ber.   No more o' that:
I prithee, do not strive against my vows.
I was compelled to her; but I lovo thee
By love's own sweet constraint and will forever   20
Do thee all rights of service.
Dia.   Ay, so you serve us
Till we serve you; but when you have our roses,
You barely leave our thorns to prick ourselves,

34. **ill:** wickedly; sinfully. Diana means that a vow to do evil is not binding even if it is sworn in the name of God Himself, since such an oath is blasphemous.

37. **unsealed:** uncertified.

And mock us with our bareness.   25

Ber.   How have I sworn!

Dia. 'Tis not the many oaths that makes the truth,
But the plain single vow that is vowed true.
What is not holy, that we swear not by,
But take the High'st to witness; then, pray you, tell   30
    me,
If I should swear by Jove's great attributes
I loved you dearly, would you believe my oaths
When I did love you ill? This has no holding,
To swear by Him whom I protest to love   35
That I will work against Him; therefore your oaths
Are words and poor, conditions but unsealed,
At least in my opinion.

Ber.   Change it, change it!
Be not so holy-cruel: love is holy;   40
And my integrity ne'er knew the crafts
That you do charge men with. Stand no more off,
But give thyself unto my sick desires,
Who then recovers. Say thou art mine, and ever
My love as it begins shall so persever.   45

Dia. I see that men may rope's in such a snare
That we'll forsake ourselves. Give me that ring.

Ber. I'll lend it thee, my dear, but have no power
To give it from me.

Dia.   Will you not, my lord?   50

Ber. It is an honor 'longing to our house,
Bequeathed down from many ancestors,
Which were the greatest obloquy i' the world
In me to lose.

Dia.   Mine honor's such a ring: 55

59. **proper:** personal.
68. **band:** bond.
77. **there:** i.e., in yielding to him without marriage, she loses hope that he will ever marry her.

My chastity's the jewel of our house,
Bequeathed down from many ancestors,
Which were the greatest obloquy i' the world
In me to lose. Thus your own proper wisdom
Brings in the champion Honor on my part   60
Against your vain assault.

   Ber.   Here, take my ring:
My house, mine honor, yea, my life, be thine,
And I'll be bid by thee.

   Dia. When midnight comes, knock at my chamber   65
     window;
I'll order take my mother shall not hear.
Now will I charge you in the band of truth,
When you have conquered my yet maiden bed,
Remain there but an hour, nor speak to me.   70
My reasons are most strong; and you shall know them
When back again this ring shall be delivered.
And on your finger in the night I'll put
Another ring, that what in time proceeds
May token to the future our past deeds.   75
Adieu, till then; then, fail not. You have won
A wife of me, though there my hope be done.

   Ber. A Heaven on earth I have won by wooing
    thee.   [*Exit.*]

   Dia. For which live long to thank both Heaven   80
    and me!
You may so in the end.
My mother told me just how he would woo,
As if she sat in 's heart. She says all men
Have the like oaths. He had sworn to marry me   85
When his wife's dead; therefore I'll lie with him

87. **braid:** deceitful.

90. **cozen:** cheat; **unjustly:** dishonestly.

━━━━━━━━━━━━━━━━━━━━━━━━━━━━━━━━━━━

IV. iii. Several French lords discuss Bertram's affairs. A letter from his mother has made a strong impression upon him. Word has also come that Helena is dead. The lords deplore Bertram's treatment of Helena and his attempts to seduce Diana. They feel that the Duke's commendation of his bravery will hardly be sufficient to offset the King's displeasure at Bertram's desertion of Helena. Bertram arrives after his supposed assignation with Diana (in reality Helena, whom he does not recognize in the dark), and the French lords bring in Parolles for questioning. On the threat of torture, Parolles reveals his knowledge of the Florentines' strength and slanders his comrades. His pocket even contains a rhymed letter warning Diana not to yield to Bertram without prior payment of money. After they have reduced Parolles to begging for his life, they remove his blindfold and reveal themselves. Disgraced in Bertram's eyes, Parolles realizes that he must now shift for himself.

━━━━━━━━━━━━━━━━━━━━━━━━━━━━━━━━━━━

5. **worthy:** deserved.

15. **fleshes his will:** gratifies his lust. The word **spoil** carries out the imagery from hunting. The hunter's hound was "fleshed" by being given a piece of the kill.

16. **monumental:** serving as a memento (the ring was a family heirloom).

17. **composition:** bargain; transaction.

80

When I am buried. Since Frenchmen are so braid,
Marry that will, I live and die a maid:
Only in this disguise I think't no sin
To cozen him that would unjustly win.   90

                                                Exit.

[Scene III. The Florentine camp.]

*Enter the two French Lords and some two or three
Soldiers.*

1. Lo. You have not given him his mother's letter?

2. Lo. I have delivered it an hour since. There is
something in't that stings his nature; for on the reading it he changed almost into another man.

1. Lo. He has much worthy blame laid upon him for   5
shaking off so good a wife and so sweet a lady.

2. Lo. Especially he hath incurred the everlasting
displeasure of the King, who had even tuned his
bounty to sing happiness to him. I will tell you a
thing, but you shall let it dwell darkly with you.   10

1. Lo. When you have spoken it, 'tis dead, and I am
the grave of it.

2. Lo. He hath perverted a young gentlewoman
here in Florence, of a most chaste renown; and this
night he fleshes his will in the spoil of her honor. He 15
hath given her his monumental ring and thinks himself made in the unchaste composition

18. **rebellion:** yielding to sin.

19. **ourselves:** i.e., naturally, without divine assistance.

20. **Merely:** absolutely.

21. **still:** always.

24. **in his proper stream o'erflows himself:** drowns (destroys) himself in the pursuit of his own course of pleasure.

25. **meant damnable:** a portent of ultimate damnation.

28-9. **dieted to his hour:** limited to an hour's meeting with Diana.

31. **company:** companion (Parolles); **anatomized:** dissected; laid bare.

32-3. **wherein so curiously he had set this counterfeit:** in which he had set this fake gem as elaborately as a precious stone.

34. **him:** Parolles; **he:** Bertram.

35. **his:** Bertram's.

44-5. **so should I be a great deal of his act:** if I were, I would share some responsibility for his actions.

47. **pretense:** intention.

1. Lo. Now, God delay our rebellion! As we are ourselves, what things are we!

2. Lo. Merely our own traitors. And as in the com- 20 mon course of all treasons we still see them reveal themselves till they attain to their abhorred ends, so he that in this action contrives against his own nobility, in his proper stream o'erflows himself.

1. Lo. Is it not meant damnable in us, to be 25 trumpeters of our unlawful intents? We shall not then have his company tonight?

2. Lo. Not till after midnight; for he is dieted to his hour.

1. Lo. That approaches apace. I would gladly have 30 him see his company anatomized, that he might take a measure of his own judgments, wherein so curiously he had set this counterfeit.

2. Lo. We will not meddle with him till he come; for his presence must be the whip of the other. 35

1. Lo. In the meantime, what hear you of these wars?

2. Lo. I hear there is an overture of peace.

1. Lo. Nay, I assure you, a peace concluded.

2. Lo. What will Count Rossillion do then? Will 40 he travel higher, or return again into France?

1. Lo. I perceive, by this demand, you are not altogether of his council.

2. Lo. Let it be forbid, sir; so should I be a great deal of his act. 45

1. Lo. Sir, his wife some two months since fled from his house: her pretense is a pilgrimage to St. Jaques le Grand; which holy undertaking with most austere

53. justified: verified.

57-8. the rector of the place: the priest who performed the last rites.

61. to the full arming of the verity: in full proof of the actuality.

sanctimony she accomplished, and, there residing,
the tenderness of her nature became as a prey to her 50
grief: in fine, made a groan of her last breath, and
now she sings in Heaven.

2. *Lo.* How is this justified?

1. *Lo.* The stronger part of it by her own letters,
which makes her story true, even to the point of her 55
death. Her death itself, which could not be her office
to say is come, was faithfully confirmed by the rector
of the place.

2. *Lo.* Hath the Count all this intelligence?

1. *Lo.* Ay, and the particular confirmations, point 60
from point, to the full arming of the verity.

2. *Lo.* I am heartily sorry that he'll be glad of this.

1. *Lo.* How mightily sometimes we make us comforts of our losses!

2. *Lo.* And how mightily some other times we 65
drown our gain in tears! The great dignity that his
valor hath here acquired for him shall at home be
encountered with a shame as ample.

1. *Lo.* The web of our life is of a mingled yarn,
good and ill together. Our virtues would be proud, if 70
our faults whipped them not; and our crimes would
despair, if they were not cherished by our virtues.

Enter a Messenger.

How now! where's your master!

Mess. He met the Duke in the street, sir, of whom
he hath taken a solemn leave: His Lordship will next 75
morning for France. The Duke hath offered him

78-9. They shall be no more than needful there, if they were more than they can commend: i.e., Bertram cannot be too highly commended to the King, if he is to regain his favor.

84. By an abstract of success: to summarize what I have accomplished.

85. congeed: exchanged formal farewells.

87-8. entertained my convoy: hired my transport.

88. parcels of dispatch: pieces of business requiring attention.

89. nicer: (1) less important; (2) more wanton.

97. module: model.

100. gallant: showily dressed.

102. usurping: assuming unrightfully (since he is a coward).

A gallant in the stocks. From Geoffrey Whitney, *A Choice of Emblems* (1586).

letters of commendations to the King.　　　*Exit.*

2. *Lo.* They shall be no more than needful there, if they were more than they can commend.

Enter Bertram.

1. *Lo.* They cannot be too sweet for the King's　80
tartness. Here's His Lordship now. How now, my
lord! is't not after midnight?

Ber. I have tonight dispatched sixteen businesses,
a month's length apiece. By an abstract of success:
I have congeed with the Duke, done my adieu with　85
his nearest, buried a wife, mourned for her, writ to
my lady mother I am returning, entertained my convoy, and between these main parcels of dispatch
effected many nicer needs. The last was the greatest,
but that I have not ended yet.　　　　90

2. *Lo.* If the business be of any difficulty, and this
morning your departure hence, it requires haste of
your Lordship.

Ber. I mean, the business is not ended, as fearing to
hear of it hereafter. But shall we have this dialogue　95
between the fool and the soldier? Come, bring forth
this counterfeit module has deceived me like a
double-meaning prophesier.

2. *Lo.* Bring him forth; has sat i' the stocks all
night, poor gallant knave.　　　　100

Ber. No matter; his heels have deserved it in
usurping his spurs so long. How does he carry himself?

2. *Lo.* I have told your Lordship already, the stocks

106. **shed:** spilled.
109. **instant:** present.
117. **Hoodman:** the blindfolded one in the game of Blindman's Bluff.
125. **out of a note:** from a list of questions.

carry him. But to answer you as you would be under- 105
stood: he weeps like a wench that had shed her milk.
He hath confessed himself to Morgan, whom he sup-
poses to be a friar, from the time of his remembrance
to this very instant disaster of his setting i' the stocks:
and what think you he hath confessed?   110

Ber. Nothing of me, has 'a?

2. Lo. His confession is taken and it shall be read to
his face. If your Lordship be in't, as I believe you are,
you must have the patience to hear it.

Enter Parolles, with his Interpreter.

Ber. A plague upon him! muffled! He can say 115
nothing of me: hush, hush!

1. Lo. Hoodman comes! *Portotartarossa.*

1. Sold. He calls for the tortures: what will you say
without 'em?

Par. I will confess what I know without constraint; 120
if ye pinch me like a pasty, I can say no more.

1. Sold. Bosko chimurcho.

1. Lo. Boblibindo chicurmurco.

1. Sold. You are a merciful general. Our general
bids you answer to what I shall ask you out of a note. 125

Par. And truly, as I hope to live.

1. Sold. [*Reads*] "First demand of him how many
horso the Duke is strong." What say you to that?

Par. Five or six thousand, but very weak and un-
serviceable: the troops are all scattered and the 130
commanders very poor rogues, upon my reputation
and credit and as I hope to live.

136. **All's one to him:** he cares for nothing.

140. **theoric:** theory.

141. **chape:** metal covering or point of a scabbard.

150. **con:** acknowledge.

150-51. **in the nature he delivers it:** i.e., seeing that he reports it traitorously.

158-59. **if I were to live this present hour:** i.e., if this hour were my last.

1. Sold. Shall I set down your answer so?

Par. Do; I'll take the sacrament on't, how and which way you will. 135

Ber. All's one to him. What a past-saving slave is this!

1. Lo. Y'are deceived, my lord: this is Monsieur Parolles, the gallant militarist—that was his own phrase—that had the whole theoric of war in the 140 knot of his scarf and the practice in the chape of his dagger.

2. Lo. I will never trust a man again for keeping his sword clean, nor believe he can have everything in him by wearing his apparel neatly. 145

1. Sold. Well, that's set down.

Par. Five or six thousand horse, I said—I will say true—or thereabouts, set down, for I'll speak truth.

1. Lo. He's very near the truth in this.

Ber. But I con him no thanks for't, in the nature 150 he delivers it.

Par. Poor rogues, I pray you, say.

1. Sold. Well, that's set down.

Par. I humbly thank you, sir; a truth's a truth, the rogues are marvelous poor. 155

1. Sold. [*Reads*] "Demand of him of what strength they are a-foot." What say you to that?

Par. By my troth, sir, if I were to live this present hour, I will tell true. Let me see: Spurio, a hundred fifty; Sebastian, so many; Corambus, so many; Jaques, 160 so many; Guiltian, Cosmo, Lodowick, and Gratii, two hundred fifty each; mine own company, Chitopher, Vaumond, Bentii, two hundred fifty each: so that the

164. **rotten and sound:** ailing and healthy.

165. **poll:** heads.

166. **cassocks:** cloaks.

183. **botcher:** clumsy shoemaker or tailor.

184-85. **the shrieve's fool:** i.e., the sheriff's idiot charge. In rural areas the mentally deficient might become wards of the sheriff.

188. **his brains are forfeit to the next tile that falls:** i.e., he deserves a speedy death. Geoffrey Whitney's *Choice of Emblems* (1586) contains an emblem that appeared earlier in one of Alciati's emblem books, showing three women who threw dice to see who would die first. The one who threw the lowest hand laughed in disbelief, but shortly afterward a tile fell from the ceiling and killed her. Lafew's reference to throwing **ames-ace** for his life in II. iii. 82–3 may derive from this same emblem.

muster-file, rotten and sound, upon my life, amounts
not to fifteen thousand poll; half of the which dare 105
not shake the snow from off their cassocks, lest they
shake themselves to pieces.

Ber. What shall be done to him?

1. Lo. Nothing, but let him have thanks. Demand
of him my condition and what credit I have with the 170
Duke.

1. Sold. Well, that's set down. [*Reads*] "You shall
demand of him whether one Captain Dumain be i'
the camp, a Frenchman; what his reputation is with
the Duke; what his valor, honesty, and expertness in 175
wars; or whether he thinks it were not possible, with
well-weighing sums of gold, to corrupt him to a revolt." What say you to this? What do you know of
it?

Par. I beseech you, let me answer to the particular 180
of the inter'gatories: demand them singly.

1. Sold. Do you know this Captain Dumain?

Par. I know him: 'a was a botcher's 'prentice in
Paris, from whence he was whipped for getting the
shrieve's fool with child—a dumb innocent, that 185
could not say him nay.

Ber. Nay, by your leave, hold your hands, though
I know his brains are forfeit to the next tile that falls.

1. Sold. Well, is this captain in the Duke of
Florence's camp?   190

Par. Upon my knowledge, he is, and lousy.

1. Lo. Nay, look not so upon me; we shall hear of
your Lordship anon.

1. Sold. What is his reputation with the Duke?

200. **In good sadness:** truthfully.
211. **proper:** handsome.
214. **ruttish:** lustful.

Par. The Duke knows him for no other but a poor 195
officer of mine and writ to me this other day to turn
him out o' the band. I think I have his letter in my
pocket.

1. Sold. Marry, we'll search.

Par. In good sadness, I do not know; either it is 200
there, or it is upon a file with the Duke's other letters
in my tent.

1. Sold. Here 'tis; here's a paper; shall I read it to
you?

Par. I do not know if it be it or no. 205

Ber. Our interpreter does it well.

1. Lo. Excellently.

1. Sold. [*Reads*] "Dian, the Count's a fool, and full
of gold"—

Par. That is not the Duke's letter, sir; that is an 210
advertisement to a proper maid in Florence, one
Diana, to take heed of the allurement of one Count
Rossillion, a foolish idle boy, but for all that very
ruttish: I pray you, sir, put it up again.

1. Sold. Nay, I'll read it first, by your favor. 215

Par. My meaning in't, I protest, was very honest in
the behalf of the maid; for I knew the young Count
to be a dangerous and lascivious boy, who is a whale
to virginity and devours up all the fry it finds.

Ber. Damnable both-sides rogue! 220

1. Sold. [*Reads*]

　　"When he swears oaths, bid him drop gold,
　　　　and take it;
　　After he scores, he never pays the score:

228. **mell:** mingle (sexually); **not to kiss:** not even worth kissing.

233-34. **with this rhyme in's forehead:** libelers were punished with the papers in which they published their libels stuck in their hatbands.

236. **armipotent:** mighty in battle.

240. **fain:** forced.

243. **nature:** my natural life.

250. **Nessus:** a centaur who attempted to rape Hercules' wife, Dejanira.

250-51. **professes:** makes a profession of; boasts of.

Nessus abducting Dejanira. From Gabriele Simeoni, *La vita et Metamorfoseo d'Ovidio* (1559).

Half won is match well made; match and
    well make it;   225
  He ne'er pays after-debts, take it before.
And say a soldier, Dian, told thee this:
Men are to mell with, boys are not to kiss.
For count of this, the Count's a fool, I know it,
Who pays before, but not when he does owe it.   230

    Thine, as he vowed to thee in thine ear,
                PAROLLES."

Ber. He shall be whipped through the army with
this rhyme in's forehead.

2. Lo. This is your devoted friend, sir, the mani- 235
fold linguist and the armipotent soldier.

Ber. I could endure anything before but a cat, and
now he's a cat to me.

1. Sold. I perceive, sir, by the general's looks, we
shall be fain to hang you.   240

Par. My life, sir, in any case: not that I am afraid
to die; but that, my offenses being many, I would repent out the remainder of nature: let me live, sir, in a
dungeon, i' the stocks, or anywhere, so I may live.

1. Sold. We'll see what may be done, so you confess 245
freely; therefore, once more to this Captain Dumain.
You have answered to his reputation with the Duke
and to his valor; what is his honesty?

Par. He will steal, sir, an egg out of a cloister. For
rapes and ravishments he parallels Nessus. He pro- 250
fesses not keeping of oaths; in breaking 'em he is
stronger than Hercules. He will lie, sir, with such
volubility that you would think truth were a fool.

269. **Mile End:** a field east of London, where the citizens trained for service with the city watch and militia; **the doubling of files:** an elementary drill.

277. **quart d'écu:** a quarter of a French crown; **fee simple:** clear title to absolute possession.

278-80. **cut the entail from all remainders, and a perpetual succession for it perpetually:** i.e., annul the right of his heirs in perpetuity to inherit.

Drunkenness is his best virtue, for he will be swine-
drunk; and in his sleep he does little harm, save to 255
his bedclothes about him; but they know his conditions and lay him in straw. I have but little more to
say, sir, of his honesty. He has everything that an
honest man should not have; what an honest man
should have, he has nothing. 260

1. Lo. I begin to love him for this.

Ber. For this description of thine honesty? A pox
upon him! For me, he's more and more a cat.

1. Sold. What say you to his expertness in war?

Par. Faith, sir, has led the drum before the English 265
tragedians: to belie him, I will not, and more of his
soldiership I know not, except, in that country he had
the honor to be the officer at a place there called
Mile End, to instruct for the doubling of files. I would
do the man what honor I can, but of this I am not 270
certain.

1. Lo. He hath out-villained villainy so far that the
rarity redeems him.

Ber. A pox on him! He's a cat still.

1. Sold. His qualities being at this poor price, I 275
need not to ask you if gold will corrupt him to revolt.

Par. Sir, for a *quart d'écu* he will sell the fee simple
of his salvation, the inheritance of it; and cut the
entail from all remainders, and a perpetual succession
for it perpetually. 280

1. Sold. What's his brother, the other Captain
Dumain?

2. Lo. Why does he ask him of me?

1. Sold. What's he?

289. lackey: a servant who ran errands afoot.

Par. E'en a crow o' the same nest; not altogether so 285
great as the first in goodness, but greater a great deal
in evil. He excels his brother for a coward, yet his
brother is reputed one of the best that is. In a retreat
he outruns any lackey; marry, in coming on he has
the cramp.   290

1. Sold. If your life be saved, will you undertake
to betray the Florentine?

Par. Ay, and the captain of his horse, Count
Rossillion.

1. Sold. I'll whisper with the general and know his 295
pleasure.

Par. [*Aside*] I'll no more drumming; a plague of all
drums! Only to seem to deserve well, and to beguile
the supposition of that lascivious young boy, the
Count, have I run into this danger. Yet who would 300
have suspected an ambush where I was taken?

1. Sold. There is no remedy, sir, but you must die.
The general says you, that have so traitorously dis-
covered the secrets of your army and made such pes-
tiferous reports of men very nobly held, can serve the 305
world for no honest use; therefore you must die.
Come, headsman, off with his head.

Par. O Lord, sir, let me live, or let me see my death!

1. Sold. That shall you, and take your leave of all
your friends.   [*Unmuffling him.*] 310
So, look about you: know you any here?

Der. Good morrow, noble Captain.

2. Lo. God bless you, Captain Parolles.

1. Lo. God save you, noble Captain.

319. **very:** absolute; complete.
336. **fooled:** made a fool of.

2. *Lo.* Captain, what greeting will you to my Lord 315
Lafew? I am for France.

1. *Lo.* Good captain, will you give me a copy of
the sonnet you writ to Diana in behalf of the Count
Rossillion? and I were not a very coward, I'd compel
it of you; but fare you well.   320

> *Exeunt [Bertram and Lords].*

1. *Sold.* You are undone, Captain; all but your scarf;
that has a knot on't yet.

Par. Who cannot be crushed with a plot?

1. *Sold.* If you could find out a country where but
women were that had received so much shame, you 325
might begin an impudent nation. Fare ye well, sir; I
am for France too: we shall speak of you there.

> *Exit, [with Soldiers].*

Par. Yet am I thankful. If my heart were great,
'Twould burst at this. Captain I'll be no more;
But I will eat and drink, and sleep as soft   330
As captain shall: simply the thing I am
Shall make me live. Who knows himself a braggart,
Let him fear this, for it will come to pass
That every braggart shall be found an ass.
Rust, sword! cool, blushes! and, Parolles, live   335
Safest in shame! Being fooled, by fool'ry thrive!
There's place and means for every man alive.
I'll after them.

> *Exit.*

IV. iv. Helena offers the Widow proof of her identity and urges that she and Diana accompany her to Marseilles, where the King is residing. From Marseilles she plans to hurry to Rossillion before Bertram's return. She warns Diana that she will have to endure some unpleasantness, but Diana is willing to assist her in any way.

23. motive: means of movement.

[Scene IV. Florence. The Widow's house.]

Enter Helena, Widow, and Diana.

Hel. That you may well perceive I have not
    wronged you,
One of the greatest in the Christian world
Shall be my surety; 'fore whose throne 'tis needful,
Ere I can perfect mine intents, to kneel.   5
Time was I did him a desired office,
Dear almost as his life; which gratitude
Through flinty Tartar's bosom would peep forth
And answer thanks. I duly am informed
His Grace is at Marseilles, to which place   10
We have convenient convoy. You must know,
I am supposed dead: the army breaking,
My husband hies him home; where, Heaven aiding,
And by the leave of my good lord the King,
We'll be before our welcome.   15
    Wid.   Gentle madam,
You never had a servant to whose trust
Your business was more welcome.
    Hel.   Nor you, mistress,
Ever a friend whose thoughts more truly labor   20
To recompense your love. Doubt not but Heaven
Hath brought me up to be your daughter's dower,
As it hath fated her to be my motive
And helper to a husband. But, O strange men!

26. **saucy:** lascivious; **cozened:** deceived.

28. **for that:** in place of that.

32. **death and honesty:** i.e., death, so that it be chaste.

35. **Yet, I pray you:** do remain mine for a while longer.

36. **with the word the time will bring on summer:** summer (an end of our trials) will be here even as we mention the word.

40. **the fine's the crown:** the proverbial saying "Mark the end" (judge a matter by its final conclusion and not before) is stated in three different ways in these lines.

IV. v. Lafew discloses to the Countess that he has requested the King to propose his daughter for Bertram's wife, which the King himself suggested when both were children. The Countess is sympathetic to the match and invites Lafew to stay with her until the King has discussed the matter with Bertram.

1-2. **snipt-taffeta:** another references to Parolles' gaudy apparel. The body and sleeves of doublets were often slashed decoratively, sometimes with fabric of another color showing through the slits.

2. **saffron:** yellow color, signifying cowardice.

3. **unbaked and doughy:** inexperienced and impressionable.

That can such sweet use make of what they hate,   25
When saucy trusting of the cozened thoughts
Defiles the pitchy night. So lust doth play
With what it loathes for that which is away.
But more of this hereafter. You, Diana,
Under my poor instructions yet must suffer   30
Something in my behalf.
    Dia.   Let death and honesty
Go with your impositions, I am yours,
Upon your will to suffer.
    Hel.   Yet, I pray you: 35
But with the word the time will bring on summer,
When briers shall have leaves as well as thorns,
And be as sweet as sharp. We must away;
Our wagon is prepared, and time revives us.
All's well that ends well: still the fine's the crown;   40
Whate'er the course, the end is the renown.
                              Exeunt.

[Scene V. Rossillion. The Count's palace.]

Enter Countess, Lafew, and [Lavatch, the] Clown.

    Lafew. No, no, no, your son was misled with a snipt-
taffeta fellow there, whose villainous saffron would
have made all the unbaked and doughy youth of a
nation in his color. Your daughter-in-law had been
alive at this hour, and your son here at home, more   5

11. **dearest:** direst.

14. **sallets:** greens.

17. **herb of grace:** another name for rue.

18-9. **not herbs . . . nose herbs:** presumably Lafew means that the two herbs mentioned are used for their scent, not for greens.

20. **Nebuchadnezzar:** see Daniel 4:25-33.

22. **Whether:** which.

30. **bauble:** a baton, used as a scepter by the professional jester, usually having a fool's head on top. As often, the word is used here in a double sense.

32. **subscribe:** testify.

Nebuchadnezzar eating grass. From Claude Menestrier, *L'art des emblèmes* (1684).

advanced by the King than by that red-tailed humble-bee I speak of.

Coun. I would I had not known him: it was the death of the most virtuous gentlewoman that ever Nature had praise for creating. If she had partaken of my flesh, and cost me the dearest groans of a mother, I could not have owed her a more rooted love.

Lafew. 'Twas a good lady, 'twas a good lady. We may pick a thousand sallets ere we light on such another herb.

Lav. Indeed, sir, she was the sweet marjoram of the salad, or rather, the herb of grace.

Lafew. They are not herbs, you knave; they are nose herbs.

Lav. I am no great Nebuchadnezzar, sir; I have not much skill in grass.

Lafew. Whether dost thou profess thyself, a knave or a fool?

Lav. A fool, sir, at a woman's service, and a knave at a man's.

Lafew. Your distinction?

Lav. I would cozen the man of his wife and do his service.

Lafew. So you were a knave at his service, indeed.

Lav. And I would give his wife my bauble, sir, to do her service.

Lafew. I will subscribe for thee, thou art both knave and fool.

Lav. At your service.

Lafew. No, no, no.

40. **fisnomy:** physiognomy; face.

42. **Black Prince:** Edward, the Black Prince, son of Edward III, who was a Devil to the French.

45. **suggest:** tempt.

51. **narrow gate:** see Matt. 5:13.

53. **chill and tender:** sensitive to cold.

63. **shrewd:** sharp; **unhappy:** doleful.

A fool with his bauble. From Stephen Batman, *The Traveled Pilgrim* (1569).
(See line 30)

Lav. Why, sir, if I cannot serve you, I can serve as great a prince as you are.

Lafew. Who's that? a Frenchman?

Lav. Faith, sir, 'a has an English name; but his fisnomy is more hotter in France than there.   40

Lafew. What prince is that?

Lav. The Black Prince, sir; alias, the Prince of Darkness; alias, the Devil.

Lafew. Hold thee, there's my purse. I give thee not this to suggest thee from thy master thou talkst of;   45 serve him still.

Lav. I am a woodland fellow, sir, that always loved a great fire; and the master I speak of ever keeps a good fire. But, sure, he is the prince of the world; let his nobility remain in 's court; I am for the house   50 with the narrow gate, which I take to be too little for pomp to enter; some that humble themselves may, but the many will be too chill and tender, and they'll be for the flow'ry way that leads to the broad gate and the great fire.   55

Lafew. Go thy ways, I begin to be aweary of thee; and I tell thee so before, because I would not fall out with thee. Go thy ways; let my horses be well looked to, without any tricks.

Lav. If I put any tricks upon 'em, sir, they shall be   60 jades' tricks; which are their own right by the law of Nature.   *Exit.*

Lafew. A shrewd knave and an unhappy.

Coun. So 'a is. My lord that's gone made himself much sport out of him. By his authority he remains   65 here, which he thinks is a patent for his sauciness;

67. he has no pace: i.e., like an unbroken horse, he has never been curbed.

73-4. out of a self-gracious remembrance: graciously, without prompting.

80. post: by post horse; speedily.

81. numbered thirty: was thirty years of age.

91. made a bold charter: boldly presumed.

and, indeed, ho has no pace but runs where he will.

Lafew. I like him well; 'tis not amiss. And I was about to tell you, since I heard of the good lady's death and that my lord your son was upon his return 70 home, I moved the King my master to speak in the behalf of my daughter; which, in the minority of them both, His Majesty, out of a self-gracious remembrance, did first propose. His Highness hath promised me to do it: and, to stop up the displeasure he hath 75 conceived against your son, there is no fitter matter. How does your Ladyship like it?

Coun. With very much content, my lord; and I wish it happily effected.

Lafew. His Highness comes post from Marseilles, of 80 as able body as when he numbered thirty. 'A will be here tomorrow, or I am deceived by him that in such intelligence hath seldom failed.

Coun. It rejoices me that I hope I shall see him ere I die. I have letters that my son will be here tonight. 85 I shall beseech your Lordship to remain with me till they meet together.

Lafew. Madam, I was thinking with what manners I might safely be admitted.

Coun. You need but plead your honorable privilege. 90

Lafew. Lady, of that I have made a bold charter; but I thank my God it holds yet.

Enter [Lavatch, the] Clown.

Lav. O madam, yonder's my lord your son with a patch of velvet on 's face. Whether there be a scar

96-7. **two pile and a half:** the best velvet was three pile (triple thickness).

99. **liv'ry:** uniform; token; **belike:** most likely.

100. **it is your carbonadoed face:** Lavatch hints that Bertram's slash resulted from the lancing of a venereal sore.

under't or no, the velvet knows; but 'tis a goodly   95
patch of velvet. His left cheek is a cheek of two pile
and a half, but his right cheek is worn bare.

Lafew. A scar nobly got, or a noble scar, is a good
liv'ry of honor; so belike is that.

Lav. But it is your carbonadoed face.   100

Lafew. Let us go see your son, I pray you. I long to
talk with the young noble soldier.

Lav. Faith, there's a dozen of 'em, with delicate fine
hats and most courteous feathers, which bow the
head and nod at every man.   105

Exeunt.

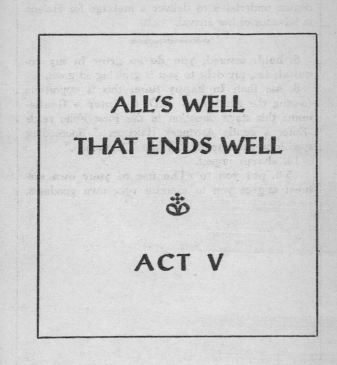

ALL'S WELL
THAT ENDS WELL

❦

ACT V

V. i. At Marseilles Helena requests the aid of a courtier in gaining admittance to the King but learns that he has already departed for Rossillion. The gentleman undertakes to deliver a message for Helena in advance of her arrival.

⬛⬛⬛⬛⬛⬛⬛⬛⬛⬛⬛⬛⬛⬛⬛

5. bold: assured; **you do so grow in my requital:** i.e., my debt to you is growing so great.

6. As: that; **In happy time:** this is opportune (seeing the gentleman). S.D. **6. Enter a Gentleman:** this stage direction in the First Folio reads "Enter a gentle Astringer [falconer]." Succeeding speech prefixes merely call him "Gentleman."

14. sharp: urgent.

15-6. put you to /The use of your own virtues: engage you to exercise your own goodness.

ACT V

[Scene I. Marseilles. A street.]

*Enter Helena, Widow, and Diana, with two
Attendants.*

Hel. But this exceeding posting day and night
Must wear your spirits low; we cannot help it.
But since you have made the days and nights as one,
To wear your gentle limbs in my affairs,
Be bold you do so grow in my requital   5
As nothing can unroot you. In happy time,

Enter a Gentleman.

This man may help me to His Majesty's ear,
If he would spend his power. God save you, sir.
  Gent. And you.
  Hel. Sir, I have seen you in the court of France.   10
  Gent. I have been sometimes there.
  Hel. I do presume, sir, that you are not fall'n
From the report that goes upon your goodness;
And therefore, goaded with most sharp occasions,
Which lay nice manners by, I put you to   15

98

35. **like:** likely.
36. **Commend:** offer.
43. **falls:** happens.

The use of your own virtues, for the which
I shall continue thankful.

    Gent.   What's your will?

    Hel. That it will please you
To give this poor petition to the King,   20
And aid me with that store of power you have
To come into his presence.

    Gent. The King's not here.

    Hel.   Not here, sir!

    Gent.   Not, indeed;   25
He hence removed last night and with more haste
Than is his use.

    Wid.   Lord, how we lose our pains!

    Hel. All's well that ends well yet—
Though time seem so adverse and means unfit.   30
I do beseech you, whither is he gone?

    Gent. Marry, as I take it, to Rossillion;
Whither I am going.

    Hel.   I do beseech you, sir,
Since you are like to see the King before me,   35
Commend the paper to his gracious hand,
Which I presume shall render you no blame
But rather make you thank your pains for it.
I will come after you with what good speed
Our means will make us means.   40

    Gent.   This I'll do for you.

    Hel. And you shall find yourself to be well thanked,
Whate'er falls more. We must to horse again.
Go, go, provide.

                              Exeunt.

V. ii. Parolles applies to Lafew for employment, and although Lafew chaffs him for a time he charitably promises him subsistence.

▓▓▓▓▓▓▓▓▓▓▓▓▓▓▓▓▓▓▓

8. fish of Fortune's butt'ring: see the proverb "Fish bred up in dirty pools will stink of mud."

8-9. allow the wind: allow me to get to windward.

17. closestool: privy.

19. pur: (1) knave (in the card game "post and pair"); (2) purr.

20. musk cat: source of musk for perfumes.

[Scene II. Rossillion. Before the Count's palace.]

Enter [Lavatch, the] Clown, and Parolles.

Par. Good Monsieur Lavatch, give my Lord Lafew
this letter. I have ere now, sir, been better known to
you, when I have held familiarity with fresher clothes;
but I am now, sir, muddied in Fortune's mood and
smell somewhat strong of her strong displeasure.   5

Lav. Truly, Fortune's displeasure is but sluttish, if
it smell so strongly as thou speakst of. I will henceforth eat no fish of Fortune's butt'ring. Prithee, allow
the wind.

Par. Nay, you need not to stop your nose, sir; I   10
spake but by a metaphor.

Lav. Indeed, sir, if your metaphor stink, I will stop
my nose; or against any man's metaphor. Prithee, get
thee further.

Par. Pray you, sir, deliver me this paper.   15

Lav. Foh! prithee, stand away: a paper from Fortune's closestool to give to a nobleman! Look, here he
comes himself.

Enter Lafew.

Here is a pur of Fortune's, sir, or of Fortune's cat—
but not a musk cat—that has fall'n into the unclean   20
fishpond of her displeasure, and, as he says, is mud-

22. **carp:** a fish that thrives in muddy ponds and sluggish streams.

23. **ingenious:** possibly for "ingenuous," meaning "well-born."

33. **let the justices make you and Fortune friends:** i.e., the justices might mend his fortunes by granting him a license to beg.

40-1. **Cox my passion:** God's passion; by the sufferings of Christ.

47. **grace:** favor.

died withal. Pray you, sir, use the carp as you may;
for he looks like a poor, decayed, ingenious, foolish,
rascally knave. I do pity his distress in my similes of
comfort and leave him to your Lordship. [*Exit.*] 25

Par. My lord, I am a man whom Fortune hath
cruelly scratched.

Lafew. And what would you have me to do? 'Tis too
late to pare her nails now. Wherein have you played
the knave with Fortune, that she should scratch you, 30
who of herself is a good lady and would not have
knaves thrive long under her? There's a *quart d'écu*
for you; let the justices make you and Fortune friends.
I am for other business.

Par. I beseech your Honor to hear me one single 35
word.

Lafew. You beg a single penny more. Come, you
shall ha't; save your word.

Par. My name, my good lord, is Parolles.

Lafew. You beg more than "word," then. Cox my 40
passion! give me your hand. How does your drum?

Par. O my good lord, you were the first that found
me!

Lafew. Was I, in sooth? And I was the first that lost
thee. 45

Par. It lies in you, my lord, to bring me in some
grace, for you did bring me out.

Lafew. Out upon thee, knave! dost thou put upon
me at once both the office of God and the Devil? One
brings thee in grace and the other brings thee out. 50
[*Trumpets sound.*] The King's coming; I know by his
trumpets. Sirrah, inquire further after me. I had talk

V. iii. The King shows himself willing to forgive Bertram, despite his treatment of Helena. Hearing that Bertram will do as he wishes in the matter of Lafew's daughter, he indicates his approval of the match. Bertram expresses his repentance and the King formally forgives his past offense. But when Bertram produces a ring as a token for Lafew's daughter, Lafew recognizes it as one that he had seen on Helena's hand. The King identifies it as one that he himself gave Helena, and his doubts about Bertram are revived, particularly after Bertram continues to deny that the ring ever belonged to his wife. Suspecting that Bertram has been responsible for Helena's death, the King orders him seized, but at that moment the gentleman sent by Helena enters and requests admittance for Diana, who seeks justice on Bertram for his seduction and desertion. Bertram denies that Diana is anything but a common strumpet with whom he whiled away the time. At length, however, Helena appears and reveals that she was Bertram's true companion, gave him the ring, and is pregnant by him. Bertram begs pardon and promises to cherish her as his wife thereafter; the King promises Diana a worthy husband and a suitable dowry.

<hr />

1. **of her:** in losing her; **esteem:** the King means that in the loss of Helena, his stock of esteem (love) has diminished, by losing one whom he esteemed so highly.

4. **home:** completely.

12. **high bent:** aimed with full force.

of you last night. Though you are a fool and a knave,
you shall eat. Go to, follow.

Par. I praise God for you.   55

[*Exeunt.*]

[Scene III. Rossillion. The Count's palace.]

*Flourish. Enter King, Countess, Lafew, the two
French Lords, with Attendants.*

King. We lost a jewel of her, and our esteem
Was made much poorer by it: but your son,
As mad in folly, lacked the sense to know
Her estimation home.

Coun.   'Tis past, my Liege;   5
And I beseech your Majesty to make it
Natural rebellion, done i' the blaze of youth,
When oil and fire, too strong for reason's force,
O'erbears it and burns on.

King.   My honored lady,   10
I have forgiven and forgotten all;
Though my revenges were high bent upon him,
And watched the time to shoot.

Lafew.   This I must say,
But first I beg my pardon, the young lord   15
Did to His Majesty, his mother, and his lady,
Offense of mighty note, but to himself
The greatest wrong of all. He lost a wife
Whose beauty did astonish the survey

20. **richest eyes:** eyes which had seen the most;
whose words all ears took captive: see illustration
symbolizing the eloquence of the Gallic Hercules,
who drew men after him by its power.

27. **The nature of his great offense is dead;**
i.e., Helena herself is dead and he will forget the
offense done her.

29. **incensing relics of it:** memories of the offense that might renew anger.

35. **hath reference to:** is referred for disposal.

40. **day of season:** seasonable day.

The Gallic Hercules and the captives of his eloquence. From
Vincenzo Cartari, *Imagini de gli dei delli antichi* (1615).

Of richest eyes, whose words all ears took captive,   20
Whose dear perfection hearts that scorned to serve
Humbly called mistress.

    King.   Praising what is lost
Makes the remembrance dear. Well, call him hither;
We are reconciled, and the first view shall kill   25
All repetition. Let him not ask our pardon;
The nature of his great offense is dead,
And deeper than oblivion we do bury
The incensing relics of it. Let him approach,
A stranger, no offender; and inform him   30
So 'tis our will he should.

    Gent.   I shall, my Liege.   *Exit.*

    King. What says he to your daughter? Have you
      spoke?

    Lafew. All that he is hath reference to your Highness.   35

    King. Then shall we have a match. I have letters
      sent me
That sets him high in fame.

Enter Count Bertram.

    Lafew.   He looks well on't.

    King. I am not a day of season,   40
For thou mayst see a sunshine and a hail
In me at once. But to the brightest beams
Distracted clouds give way. So stand thou forth;
The time is fair again.

    Ber.   My high-repented blames,   45
Dear sovereign, pardon to me.

    King.   All is whole;

49. let's take the instant by the forward top: a rephrasing of the proverb "Take Time by the forelock, for he is bald behind."

58. perspective: distorting glass.

59. favor: facial appearance.

60. expressed it stol'n: i.e., adjudged it artificial.

63. she: Helena.

68. compt: account.

69. remorseful: compassionate.

Taking Occasion (the instant) by the "forward top." From Jean Jacques Boissard, *Emblematum liber* (1588).

Not one word more of the consumed time.
Let's take the instant by the forward top;
For we are old, and on our quick'st decrees   50
The inaudible and noiseless foot of Time
Steals ere we can effect them. You remember
The daughter of this lord?

   Ber. Admiringly, my Liege. At first
I stuck my choice upon her, ere my heart   55
Durst make too bold a herald of my tongue;
Where, the impression of mine eye infixing,
Contempt his scornful perspective did lend me,
Which warped the line of every other favor,
Scorned a fair color, or expressed it stol'n,   60
Extended or contracted all proportions
To a most hideous object. Thence it came
That she whom all men praised and whom myself,
Since I have lost, have loved, was in mine eye
The dust that did offend it.   65

   King.   Well excused.
That thou didst love her strikes some scores away
From the great compt; but love that comes too late,
Like a remorseful pardon slowly carried,
To the great sender turns a sour offense,   70
Crying "That's good that's gone." Our rash faults
Make trivial price of serious things we have,
Not knowing them until we know their grave.
Oft our displeasures, to ourselves unjust,
Destroy our friends and after weep their dust;   75
Our own love, waking, cries to see what's done,
While shameful hate sleeps out the afternoon.

84. **cess:** variant form of "cease."
86. **favor:** gift.
100. **reave:** rob.
101. **stead:** assist.
103. **take it so:** so identify it.

Be this sweet Helen's knell, and now forget her.
Send forth your amorous token for fair Maudlin.
The main consents are had; and here we'll stay   80
To see our widower's second marriage day.

   Coun. Which better than the first, O dear Heaven,
     bless!
Or, ere they meet, in me, O nature, cess!

   Lafew. Come on, my son, in whom my house's name   85
Must be digested, give a favor from you
To sparkle in the spirits of my daughter,
That she may quickly come.   [*Bertram gives a ring.*]
                By my old beard,
And ev'ry hair that's on't, Helen, that's dead,   90
Was a sweet creature: such a ring as this,
The last that e'er I took her leave at court,
I saw upon her finger.

   Ber.   Hers it was not.

   King. Now, pray you, let me see it; for mine eye,   95
While I was speaking, oft was fastened to't.
This ring was mine; and, when I gave it Helen,
I bade her, if her fortunes ever stood
Necessitied to help, that by this token
I would relieve her. Had you that craft, to reave her   100
Of what should stead her most?

   Ber.   My gracious sovereign,
Howe'er it pleases you to take it so,
The ring was never hers.

   Coun.   Son, on my life,   105
I have seen her wear it; and she reckoned it
At her life's rate.

113-14. subscribed /To mine own fortune: testified as to my condition; i.e., that he was married.

117. heavy satisfaction: sorrowful understanding.

119. Plutus: god of wealth.

120. tinct and multiplying med'cine: the alchemical formula for changing base metal into gold.

121. science: knowledge.

130. Upon her great disaster: in a time of great trouble.

An alchemist experimenting. From Konrad Gesner, *The New Jewel of Health* (1576).

Lafew.   I am sure I saw her wear it.

Ber. You are deceived, my lord; she never saw it.
In Florence was it from a casement thrown me,   110
Wrapped in a paper which contained the name
Of her that threw it. Noble she was, and thought
I stood engaged; but when I had subscribed
To mine own fortune and informed her fully
I could not answer in that course of honor   115
As she had made the overture, she ceased
In heavy satisfaction and would never
Receive the ring again.

King.   Plutus himself,
That knows the tinct and multiplying med'cine,   120
Hath not in nature's mystery more science
Than I have in this ring. 'Twas mine, 'twas Helen's,
Whoever gave it you. Then, if you know
That you are well acquainted with yourself,
Confess 'twas hers and by what rough enforcement   125
You got it from her. She called the saints to surety
That she would never put it from her finger,
Unless she gave it to yourself in bed,
Where you have never come, or sent it us
Upon her great disaster.   130

Ber.   She never saw it.

King. Thou speakst it falsely, as I love mine honor,
And makest conjectural fears to come into me
Which I would fain shut out. If it should prove
That thou art so inhuman—'twill not prove so—   135
And yet I know not: thou didst hate her deadly,
And she is dead; which nothing, but to close
Her eyes myself, could win me to believe,

140-42. **My forepassed proofs, howe'er the matter fall, /Shall tax my fears of little vanity, /Having vainly feared too little:** however this matter turns out, the previous evidence I have seen is sufficient to acquit my fears of folly, having in the past foolishly feared too little.

152. **for four or five removes come short:** i.e., failed to overtake the King at four or five of his stops.

153. **tender:** offer.

156-57. **Her business looks in her /With an importing visage:** her manner proclaims important business.

158. **brief:** report.

159. **with:** i.e., equally with.

More than to see this ring. Take him away.

[*Guards seize Bertram.*]

My forepassed proofs, howe'er the matter fall,   140
Shall tax my fears of little vanity,
Having vainly feared too little. Away with him!
We'll sift this matter further.

Ber.   If you shall prove
This ring was ever hers, you shall as easy   145
Prove that I husbanded her bed in Florence,
Where yet she never was.   [*Exit, guarded.*]

Enter a Gentleman.

King. I am wrapped in dismal thinkings.
Gent.   Gracious sovereign,
Whether I have been to blame or no, I know not: 150
Here's a petition from a Florentine,
Who hath for four or five removes come short
To tender it herself. I undertook it,
Vanquished thereto by the fair grace and speech
Of the poor suppliant, who by this I know   155
Is here attending. Her business looks in her
With an importing visage; and she told me,
In a sweet verbal brief, it did concern
Your Highness with herself.

King. [*Reads*] "Upon his many protestations to 160
marry me when his wife was dead, I blush to say it,
he won me. Now is the Count Rossillion a widower:
his vows are forfeited to me, and my honor's paid to
him. He stole from Florence, taking no leave, and I

169. **toll:** pay a toll (to get rid of).
171. **on:** of.
178. **sith:** since.
179. **swear them lordship:** promise them marriage.

follow him to his country for justice. Grant it me, O 165
King! In you it best lies; otherwise a seducer flourishes
and a poor maid is undone.

DIANA CAPILET."

Lafew. I will buy me a son-in-law in a fair, and toll
for this. I'll none of him.   170

King. The Heavens have thought well on thee,
        Lafew,
To bring forth this discov'ry. Seek these suitors.
Go speedily and bring again the Count.

[*Exit Gentleman.*]

I am afeard the life of Helen, lady,   175
Was foully snatched.

Coun.   Now, justice on the doers!

[*Enter Bertram, guarded.*]

King. I wonder, sir, sith wives are monsters to you,
And that you fly them as you swear them lordship,
Yet you desire to marry.   180

Enter Widow and Diana.

What woman's that?

Dia. I am, my lord, a wretched Florentine,
Derived from the ancient Capilet.
My suit, as I do understand, you know,
And therefore know how far I may be pitied.   185

Wid. I am her mother, sir, whose age and honor
Both suffer under this complaint we bring,

199. **embodied yours:** made one with you.
204. **fond and desp'rate:** desperately fond.
209. **you have them ill to friend:** you have their hostility.
217. **gamester:** strumpet.

And both shall cease, without your remedy.

    King. Come hither, Count. Do you know these
    women?   190

    Ber. My lord, I neither can nor will deny
But that I know them. Do they charge me further?

    Dia. Why do you look so strange upon your wife?

    Ber. She's none of mine, my lord.

    Dia.   If you shall marry, 195
You give away this hand, and that is mine;
You give away Heaven's vows, and those are mine;
You give away myself, which is known mine;
For I by vow am so embodied yours,
That she which marries you must marry me,   200
Either both or none.

    Lafew. Your reputation comes too short for my
daughter; you are no husband for her.

    Ber. My lord, this is a fond and desp'rate creature
Whom sometime I have laughed with: let your High- 205
    ness
Lay a more noble thought upon mine honor
Than for to think that I would sink it here.

    King. Sir, for my thoughts, you have them ill to friend
Till your deeds gain them. Fairer prove your honor 210
Than in my thought it lies.

    Dia.   Good my lord,
Ask him upon his oath if he does think
He had not my virginity.

    King. What sayst thou to her?   215

    Ber.   She's impudent, my lord,
And was a common gamester to the camp.

221. **respect:** valuation; **validity:** worth.

227. **sequent issue;** succeeding heir.

228. **owed:** possessed.

237. **quoted:** reputed.

238. **taxed and deboshed:** criticized for being debauched.

244. **boarded:** accosted.

245. **her distance:** i.e., like a fencer, she knew how to keep him at the proper distance for safety.

Dia. He does me wrong, my lord. If I were so,
He might have bought me at a common price.
Do not believe him. O, behold this ring,   220
Whose high respect and rich validity
Did lack a parallel; yet for all that
He gave it to a commoner o' the camp,
If I be one.
    Coun. He blushes, and 'tis hit.   225
Of six preceding ancestors, that gem,
Conferred by testament to the sequent issue,
Hath it been owed and worn. This is his wife:
That ring's a thousand proofs.
    King.   Methought you said   230
You saw one here in court could witness it.
    Dia. I did, my lord, but loath am to produce
So bad an instrument: his name's Parolles.
    Lafew. I saw the man today, if man he be.
    King. Find him and bring him hither.   235
                                    [*Exit an Attendant.*]
    Ber.   What of him?
He's quoted for a most perfidious slave,
With all the spots o' the world taxed and deboshed;
Whose nature sickens but to speak a truth.
Am I or that or this for what he'll utter,   240
That will speak anything?
    King.   She hath that ring of yours.
    Ber. I think she has: certain it is I liked her,
And boarded her i' the wanton way of youth.
She knew her distance and did angle for me,   245
Madding my eagerness with her restraint,

247. **fancy's:** love's.

248. **motives:** movers.

249-50. **Her infinite cunning, with her modern grace, /Subdued me to her rate:** i.e., it was her infinite cunning as much as her charm, which is only commonplace, that won him to agree to her price.

255. **diet:** dismiss with a day's pay, from Medieval Latin *dieta*, meaning a day's work or wage.

269. **boggle shrewdly:** waver sharply.

As all impediments in fancy's course
Are motives of more fancy; and, in fine,
Her infinite cunning, with her modern grace,
Subdued me to her rate. She got the ring;   250
And I had that which any inferior might
At market price have bought.

    Dia.   I must be patient.
You, that have turned off a first so noble wife,
May justly diet me. I pray you yet—   255
Since you lack virtue I will lose a husband—
Send for your ring, I will return it home,
And give me mine again.

    Ber.   I have it not.

    King. What ring was yours, I pray you?   260

    Dia.   Sir, much like
The same upon your finger.

    King. Know you this ring? This ring was his of late.

    Dia. And this was it I gave him, being abed.

    King. The story then goes false you threw it him   265
Out of a casement.

    Dia.   I have spoke the truth.

           Enter Parolles.

    Ber. My lord, I do confess the ring was hers.

    King. You boggle shrewdly, every feather starts
      you.   270
Is this the man you speak of?

    Dia.   Ay, my lord.

    King. Tell me, sirrah—but tell me true, I charge
      you,

276. **on your just proceeding:** provided that you deal honestly.

277. **By:** about.

290. **equivocal companion:** evasive fellow.

293-94. **a good drum . . . but a naughty orator:** i.e., noisy but untruthful.

303. **motions:** proposals.

Not fearing the displeasure of your master,   275
Which on your just proceeding I'll keep off—
By him and by this woman here what know you?

Par. So please your Majesty, my master hath been
an honorable gentleman: tricks he hath had in him
which gentlemen have.   280

King. Come, come, to the purpose. Did he love this
woman?

Par. Faith, sir, he did love her; but how?

King. How, I pray you?

Par. He did love her, sir, as a gentleman loves a   285
woman.

King. How is that?

Par. He loved her, sir, and loved her not.

King. As thou art a knave and no knave. What an
equivocal companion is this!   290

Par. I am a poor man, and at your Majesty's command.

Lafew. He's a good drum, my lord, but a naughty
orator.

Dia. Do you know he promised me marriage?   295

Par. Faith, I know more than I'll speak.

King. But wilt thou not speak all thou knowst?

Par. Yes, so please your Majesty. I did go between
them, as I said; but more than that, he loved her: for
indeed he was mad for her, and talked of Satan, and   300
of Limbo, and of Furies, and I know not what. Yet
I was in that credit with them at that time that I knew
of their going to bed, and of other motions, as promising her marriage, and things which would derive me

308. **fine:** circumspect; subtle.
332. **customer:** prostitute.

ill will to speak of; therefore I will not speak what I   305
know.

King. Thou hast spoken all already, unless thou
canst say they are married: but thou art too fine in
thy evidence; therefore stand aside.
This ring, you say, was yours?   310
 Dia.   Ay, my good lord.
 King. Where did you buy it? or who gave it you?
 Dia. It was not given me, nor I did not buy it.
 King. Who lent it you?
 Dia.   It was not lent me neither.   315
 King. Where did you find it, then?
 Dia.   I found it not.
 King. If it were yours by none of all these ways,
How could you give it him?
 Dia.   I never gave it him.   320
 Lafew. This woman's an easy glove, my lord: she
goes off on at pleasure.
 King. This ring was mine; I gave it his first wife.
 Dia. It might be yours or hers, for aught I know.
 King. Take her away. I do not like her now.   325
To prison with her; and away with him.
Unless thou tellst me where thou hadst this ring,
Thou diest within this hour.
 Dia.   I'll never tell you.
 King. Take her away.   330
 Dia.   I'll put in bail, my Liege.
 King. I think thee now some common customer.
 Dia. By Jove, if ever I knew man, 'twas you.
 King. Wherefore hast thou accused him all this
  while?   335

344. **surety:** certify; vouch for.
350. **quick:** (1) alive; (2) pregnant.
352. **exorcist:** conjurer.
353. **Beguiles:** deceives.

Dia. Because he's guilty, and he is not guilty.
He knows I am no maid, and he'll swear to't;
I'll swear I am a maid, and he knows not.
Great King, I am no strumpet, by my life:
I am either maid, or else this old man's wife.   340
     King. She does abuse our ears; to prison with her.
     Dia. Good mother, fetch my bail. Stay, royal sir:
                              [*Exit Widow.*]
The jeweler that owes the ring is sent for,
And he shall surety me. But for this lord,
Who hath abused me, as he knows himself,   345
Though yet he never harmed me, here I quit him.
He knows himself my bed he hath defiled;
And at that time he got his wife with child.
Dead though she be, she feels her young one kick.
So there's my riddle: One that's dead is quick.   350
And now behold the meaning.

               Enter Helena and Widow.

     King.   Is there no exorcist
Beguiles the truer office of mine eyes?
Is 't real that I see?
     Hel.   No, my good lord;   355
'Tis but the shadow of a wife you see,
The name and not the thing.
     Ber.   Both, both. O, pardon!
     Hel. O my good lord, when I was like this maid,
I found you wondrous kind. There is your ring;   360
And, look you, here's your letter: this it says:
"When from my finger you can get this ring

381. honest: chaste.

384. Resolvedly more leisure shall express: the details shall be resolved when time permits.

And are by me with child," etc. This is done.
Will you be mine, now you are doubly won?

   Ber. If she, my Liege, can make me know this   365
   clearly,
I'll love her dearly, ever, ever dearly.

   Hel. If it appear not plain and prove untrue,
Deadly divorce step between me and you!
O my dear mother, do I see you living?   370

   Lafew. Mine eyes smell onions: I shall weep anon.
[*To Parolles*] Good Tom Drum, lend me a hand-
kercher. So, I thank thee. Wait on me home, I'll make
sport with thee. Let thy curtsies alone, they are
scurvy ones.   375

   King. Let us from point to point this story know,
To make the even truth in pleasure flow.
[*To Diana*] If thou beest yet a fresh uncropped
   flower,
Choose thou thy husband, and I'll pay thy dower;   380
For I can guess that by thy honest aid
Thou keptst a wife herself, thyself a maid.
Of that and all the progress, more and less,
Resolvedly more leisure shall express.
All yet seems well; and if it end so meet,   385
The bitter past, more welcome is the sweet. *Flourish.*

Epil. 5. Ours be your patience then, and yours our parts: i.e., we, the actors, change places with you, the audience, to witness how you will end the play—with applause or disapproval.

[*EPILOGUE*]

King. The King's a beggar, now the play is done.
All is well ended, if this suit be won,
That you express content; which we will pay,
With strife to please you, day exceeding day.
Ours be your patience then, and yours our parts; 5
Your gentle hands lend us, and take our hearts.

                              [*Exeunt omnes.*]

'Twere all one
That I should love a bright particular star
And think to wed it, he is so above me.   [*Helena*—I.i.90-2]

Withal, full oft we see
Cold wisdom waiting on superfluous folly.
[*Helena*—I.i.110-11]

Our remedies oft in ourselves do lie,
Which we ascribe to Heaven: the fated sky
Gives us free scope, only doth backward pull
Our slow designs when we ourselves are dull.
[*Helena*—I.i.222-25]

He must needs go that the Devil drives. [*Lavatch*—I.iii.29-30]

If ever we are Nature's, these are ours; this thorn
Doth to our rose of youth rightly belong;
Our blood to us, this to our blood is born.
[*Countess*—I.iii.129-31]

'Tis often seen,
Adoption strives with nature; and choice breeds
A native slip to us from foreign seeds.
[*Countess*—I.iii.146-48]

Thus, Indian-like,
Religious in mine error, I adore
The sun, that looks upon his worshiper
But knows of him no more.   [*Helena*—I.iii.214-17]

Good alone
Is good without a name; vileness is so.
The property by what it is should go,
Not by the title.   [*King* II.iii.130-42]

The web of our life is of a mingled yarn, good
and ill together.   [*First Lord*—IV.iii.69-70]

All's well that ends well: still the fine's the crown;
Whate'er the course, the end is the renown.
[*Helena*—IV.iv.40-1]

Whose words all ears took captive.   [*Lafew*—V.iii.20]